SISTERS
IN ZION

SISTERS
IN ZION

Hope and Inspiration for Women

Marilynne Todd Linford

Covenant Communications, Inc.

Cover illustration *Tamed* © Anita Robbins.

Cover design copyrighted 2005 by Covenant Communications, Inc.

Published by Covenant Communications, Inc.
American Fork, Utah

Printed in Canada
First Printing: April 2005

11 10 09 08 07 06 05   10 9 8 7 6 5 4 3 2 1

ISBN 1-59156-872-2

To my mother,
who lives life with energy, enthusiasm, and empathy

TABLE OF CONTENTS

INTRODUCTION

Four years ago, my Relief Society president came to me with a proposal. She expressed concern that the younger mothers didn't have the advantage, as we did, of mother-education lessons that were once part of the Relief Society curriculum. She asked if I would write a mother-education lesson each month that would be printed on the back of the visiting teaching message to be left in the homes of the sisters. She agreed to give me a list of topics, and I enthusiastically agreed to write the lessons if I could remain anonymous. I felt the teachings would be more effective if no one knew who authored them. (The approach has changed a little for the purposes of publication.) Nevertheless, the plan worked, and the ward sisters were receptive. But as the lessons emerged, I noticed that most of the lessons were not specifically for mothers, because all women can inspire children, and the lessons were basically the gospel in action—which can apply to everyone. I even hoped husbands and fathers would read certain chapters. As the months became years, I heard that some of the sisters were compiling the lessons and sending them to their daughters, which gave me the idea for this book—*Sisters in Zion*. I do want you to know that the *Hope and Inspiration* part was the publisher's idea, because I can't take credit for any of the ideas. What I didn't learn from my mother, I learned from my Relief Society sisters—that's you! Thank you for the way you nurture your children. Thank you for the way you hurdle life's obstacles. And thank you for your example, your understanding, your friendship, and love.

To set the stage before the curtain goes up on this book, I've thought about the hymn "As Sisters in Zion" (*Hymns,* 309). I love the classic language of Emily H. Woodmansee (1836–1906) and hope I'm not detracting from her lyrical poetry. I simply want to add my testimony to hers of the privilege of being a sister in Zion. The following lines are my addition written in the spirit of the song:

> As sisters in Zion, we learn from each other.
> Through visiting teaching and friendships we share
> The truths of the gospel and provident living.
> We show love to God, for each sister we care.
>
> As sisters in Zion, we honor the priesthood
> That through temple blessings we're privileged to share.
> We know that God's voice can be heard in the scriptures
> And through living prophets His truth is declared.
>
> As sisters in Zion, we pray for more wisdom
> In these latter-days to keep covenants revealed.
> We want to be valiant, courageous, and steadfast,
> Inheriting blessings to which we've been sealed.
>
> As sisters in Zion, we treasure the calling
> Of bearing and nurturing children of God.
> We love them and teach them and earnestly pray
> That with firmness they'll cling to the Lord's iron rod.

CELEBRATING PEOPLE

I am good at celebrating events such as Christmas, the Fourth of July, Thanksgiving, Easter, Labor Day, and Memorial Day. Sometimes I remember that I'm actually celebrating people in those events—Christ on Easter and Christmas, the founding fathers on the Fourth of July, the pilgrims on Thanksgiving, those who labor on Labor Day, and those who have passed away, especially in defense of our country, on Memorial Day. As important as celebrating holidays and people of the past, is celebrating the real, living people in my life by remembering births, baptisms, birthdays, graduations, marriages, anniversaries, retirements, and deaths. Personal milestones and anniversaries deserve to be observed. Celebrating events is good; celebrating people is better.

Celebrating children is a glorious opportunity. Today is most likely not the birthday or graduation or anniversary of anyone in your home. Today is probably not a state or national holiday, but there is much celebrating that can be done within your nuclear family. Think of each child who calls you mother. No matter how many children you have, each of them has only one mother. What would happen if you individually celebrated each child every day?

A mother shared her attempt at celebrating. "I know that some of the problems in my home have come as result of not enough people-celebrating. I am a lot better at criticizing than praising. Sometimes I have felt barriers like prison walls between a child and me. During an especially difficult time, I prayed for a way to improve such a situation. A simple idea came. Each time I saw that child, I smiled at him. I couldn't praise him; he wouldn't accept it. But I could smile. This simple gesture repeated over and over helped melt the barrier between us."

Another very simple form of celebration is to use the child's name with respect. A child's name is his or her identity. Some mothers use the child's full name only when he or she is in trouble. Save using his or her full name for times of praise and celebration.

Another simple form of celebrating is saying thanks and showing appreciation. "I noticed you let Laura do the puzzle with you." "Congratulations on missing only three spelling words." "I enjoy hearing you practice." According to tradition, the Duke of Wellington was asked near the end of his life what he would have done differently. He said, "I would have given more praise." Celebrating events is good; celebrating people is better; celebrating the people closest to you is best.

Celebrating our husbands is another area we might be lax in. I don't feel I am good enough at husband-celebrating. I try to regularly tell my husband that I appreciate the good things he does, but I take so much for granted. I've watched married couples whose communication has deteriorated into sarcasm and criticism. I don't want that kind of marriage. The way I avoid falling into that habit is by the "rule of three," which is that I try to leave three unkind things unsaid and to replace them with three kind things every day. Do you celebrate your husband enough? If you have a tendency to find fault with him, try using the rule of three. Making time for your husband is also a good way to show appreciation for him. Friday-night dates are a great form of celebration for couples, whether in their first month or sixtieth year of marriage.

There are times in most marriages when the husband and wife feel incongruous and disharmonious with each other. Celebrating marriage and remembering covenants make these times of frustration less exasperating and help smooth out points of friction. There are legitimate differences that sometimes need expression in marriage and that couples must take time to work through. But quiet communication does much more for the marriage than yelling, name-calling, and discussing problems with outsiders. Quiet communication with empathy is a great way to celebrate your marriage.

I've known couples that divorced who seemed well suited for each other. I've seen others who seemed mismatched, yet end up with happy marriages. Why? I think it is a matter of commitment to marriage as an institution, a matter of making a decision to celebrate one's spouse. In my experience, it's not always a joint decision to make the marriage work. In many cases, one spouse decides to save the marriage by telling his or her spouse through actions and words, "You are the one with whom I want to spend the rest of this life and eternity. I would choose you again. I'm in this for the long haul." You can be the one who makes changes in your marriage when it seems things are headed downhill.

Even if you have dissimilarities that need resolution, you can still consciously decide to love your spouse. Love isn't something over which you have no control. Love is not something you fall in and out of. Love is a decision. Daily deciding to love your husband is celebrating your marriage covenant and celebrating him. Celebrating the person with whom you said "I do!" is the best choice you can make for your family.

In particular, celebrating your husband as the father of your children will help your children love their father. Never speak negatively about him in hearing range of your children. Husband bashing is a popular sport. "See what I have to deal with" is the topic du jour in the workplace and in telephone conversations between female friends and family. This is destructive to children who hear you. Your boys need a high image of their father to appreciate their own masculinity. Girls need a positive impression of their father and wholesome interactions with him to give them a healthy attitude toward men.

All men have faults. If the father's faults are paraded before the children, irreparable damage is done three ways—to the wife and mother, whose negative focus is mocking, belittling, and sometimes even vilifying the man who should be the most important person in her life; to the children, who see their father and themselves (they are half his) through their mother's disapproving eyes; and to the husband, who will live up (or down) to the expectations placed on him.

How blessed is the family in which the mother models healthy behavior and teaches her children to honor their father. As a natural outcome, children will thereby honor their mother, and the priesthood of God that fathers bear is also honored.

Here are three practical ways to celebrate your husband as your children's father:

1. Acknowledge his importance by including him in the children's lives. When a child asks for permission to do something, go somewhere, or get something, say, "Let's talk to Dad." And then support his decision or that which was agreed upon. (Don't include their father in the decision-making process unless you will not interfere in whatever decision he makes.) In many homes, mothers make all the decisions, and fathers are expected to be good sports and follow along, much like one of the children. This is not representative of the partnership marriage should be.

2. Remind the children of the good things their father does for the family. "Wasn't that nice of Daddy to fix your bike?" "Dad is getting off early from work to be at your game." "Your dad goes to work every day to earn money so that we can live in this nice house, have food to eat, clothes to wear, and toys to play with."

3. Celebrate your children's father by celebrating his homecomings, as is learned in the Primary song lyrics, "I'm so glad when Daddy comes home" ("Daddy's Homecoming," *Children's Songbook,* 210). Make Daddy's homecoming a daily celebration—not so that he can help with the work, but because he's loved.

In a perfect world, celebrating each other could save all marriages, and all family relationships would be amicable. But because of sin and extreme selfishness (which are most often evidenced in the three *A*'s—*addiction, abuse, adultery*), a woman may have no choice *but* to divorce. Many women in the Church rear children alone and also assume the breadwinner role—*not* because they didn't try hard enough and *not* because they didn't have a strong enough testimony of the importance of marriage. Most of them do what they do because they have no other option. These women struggle. Life is lonely for them. They have to do it all alone. Is there anyone to celebrate them? Not the ex-spouse. Not usually the children. Not society in general. (Have you seen many greeting cards that say, "Congratulations on your divorce!") But there is a form of celebration, established by the Lord, in which all women can participate. That's what Relief Society is—an organization where sisters seek out other sisters and show their appreciation and love. It's a celebration organization where I need you and you need me. Just today I felt celebrated by one of my Relief Society sisters. My visiting teacher brought me six oatmeal raisin cookies. She said she was thinking about me today and wanted me to know it. Who doesn't appreciate being celebrated, especially with an oatmeal cookie? To keep your priorities straight, however, if you celebrate your Relief Society sisters better and more often than the people you live with, repair the disparity. Celebrate life's events, celebrate the people in your life, including your Relief Society sisters, but do your best celebrating of and with those in your home!

CHARITY: WHAT IT IS, HOW TO GET IT, AND HOW IT MAKES EVERYTHING BETTER

One Christmastime, about three years before he succumbed to leukemia, Elder Neal A. Maxwell spoke to a group in the Church Office Building in Salt Lake City. He greeted each of us at the door and spoke kind words. He was tired and thin in body, giant in spirit. As part of his remarks after dinner, he told of his experiences with fatigue and suffering. He explained that some nights he would literally drop into bed, wondering if he had the strength to turn over, when he'd remember, *I am an Apostle of Jesus Christ*. According to my memory, he would then pray something along these lines: "Heavenly Father, is there something else I need to do today before I retire for the night?" If an idea came, he'd collect the courage to get up and do whatever was needed. He spoke intimately of Jesus Christ and of his desire to serve as Christ served.

To achieve this level of understanding of the pure love of Christ, and to try to emulate it to that degree, may be daunting. However, it is an attainable goal. If we learn what it is, like any principle of the gospel, we will better understand it, enabling us to learn how to develop it.

To understand what charity is, let us consider three concepts. First, charity is a gift of the Spirit (see Bruce R. McConkie, *Mormon Doctrine*, 121). Since charity is a gift of the Spirit, how can I receive it? There may be those persons who are born with the gift of charity, as some are born with the gift of testimony or tongues or healing. But if it comes like a testimony does, I can do my part—desire it, study about it, pray, fast, and wait—but charity is the Lord's to give. I think charity comes much like testimony, line upon line. Most likely the most important aspects of the process are to ask Heavenly Father in prayer for the gift of charity, to try to emulate Jesus Christ, who embodies all charity, and to listen for and obey promptings from the Holy Ghost.

Second, charity is more than just a "manifestation of love." Charity is "devoid of all desire for praise or hope of return." It is "the love that suffers long; that envies not others; that vaunts not itself; that knows no pride; that subdues selfishness; that rejoices in the truth" (James E. Talmage, *Articles of Faith*, 432–33).

We can learn about this aspect of charity by observing the Savior in the way He cared for others. His treatment of the woman who had the issue of blood for twelve years is a good example. In that brief interaction, Christ's charity is shown (see Matt. 9:20–22; Mark 5:25–34; Luke 8:43–48).

He was busy, en route to somewhere else. Yet He could feel the need of the one in a throng.

He was on a critical errand. Jairus had asked Him to come bless his daughter, who was "at the point of death" (Mark 5:23). But He stopped when He felt the woman reach out to Him (v. 30).

He was in the company of a ruler of the synagogue (Matt. 9:18; Luke 8:41). The fact that the ruler had prestige and the woman was unclean made no difference. He willingly stopped and performed the miracle for her.

Could it be that one reason for this miracle at that moment was to strengthen the faith of Jairus so that he too could have the miracle he desired? Sometimes more than one good thing can be accomplished with the same charitable act.

Jesus cured not only her physical distress, but her ostracism and loneliness; Jesus cures physical and emotional illnesses.

He acknowledged her faith and taught the multitude that faith in Him can make us whole. "Jesus turned him about, and when he saw her, he said, Daughter, be of good comfort; thy faith hath made thee whole. And the woman was made whole from that hour" (Matt. 9:22).

Charity can be done in many ways. For example, some may conclude from Mother Teresa's example that acts of charity must be done in some magnificent way, such as in going to India. However, there's a story told about Mother Teresa from when she first arrived in

India as a young nun. As the story goes, she looked around at the millions of people living in squalor and disease and was terrified at the magnitude of need. It is said that she prayed to be sent somewhere else. The needs were just too great, and she was only one little woman. According to tradition, as she said this prayer, asking for another assignment, a voice said, "Minister to the one nearest to you" (*Mother Teresa, a Life of Devotion* [A&E Home Video: 1997], BBC). Charity can be given or offered anytime, anywhere. Use your charity to minister to the one nearest you—both in relationship and proximity—and it's most likely not in India. It's probably within the four walls you call home.

One important lesson of "ministering to the one closest to you" is often overlooked. *You* are the one closest to you. When your needs conflict with another's immediate needs, what should you do? Ask in prayer for guidance and listen for promptings. That's how you'll know. The truest answer to how much of yourself is required is however much the Lord asks.

There will be times that you follow the Lord's promptings and with charity do what you were led to do, and the Spirit will whisper, "It's enough. Go get some sleep." Obey the Spirit. It is so easy to let the natural woman in you say, "Wow! That charity experience felt good. I'm going to do this and that and another thing." And you disobey, exhausting yourself. Several scriptures warn about running faster than you have strength (see D&C 10:4). You must take care of yourself. You are the first line of charity for the person closest to you—you. How does this work? With the Holy Ghost as your guide, sometimes you dig deep down and find there is more to give than you thought; sometimes you balance and prioritize and sacrifice; sometimes you find help coming from unexpected sources; and sometimes you find that your needs are filled as you fill others' needs. There will be times you know it is pride or vanity or some other "natural woman" excuse that's prodding you on and not the Spirit; there will be times you will know you are to "rest from your labors [for a season]" (D&C 59:10), and, in so doing, regroup, recoup, recover, regain, and reorganize.

A third point about charity is that of faith, hope, and charity, it is the greatest (see 1 Cor. 13:13 and Moro. 7:44). Women who possess the gift of charity know that charity will never fail. It cannot. Charity will never fail because "charity is the pure love of Christ, and it endureth forever" (Moro. 7:47). Charity will not fail because Christ will not fail. Moroni quotes the monumental words of his father, Mormon:

> Wherefore, my beloved brethren, if ye have not charity, ye are nothing, for charity never faileth. Wherefore, cleave unto charity, which is the greatest of all, for all things must fail—But charity is the pure love of Christ, and it endureth forever; and whoso is found possessed of it at the last day, it shall be well with him. Wherefore, my beloved brethren, pray unto the Father with all the energy of heart, that ye may be filled with this love, which he hath bestowed upon all who are true followers of his Son, Jesus Christ; that ye may become the sons of God; that when he shall appear we shall be like him, for we shall see him as he is; that we may have this hope; that we may be purified even as he is pure. (Moro. 7:46–48)

COMMUNICATION:
BROADCASTING THE
CONVERSATIONS IN YOUR HOME

Using a weather analogy, if there were a thermometer and a barometer displayed on the outside of your home giving a constant readout of the communications happening within, what would be the forecast? In one house, "cloudy and stormy with cold temperatures" might be the predictable weather pattern day after day, "rays of sunshine and blue skies being unusual." One woman described the weather pattern in her house as "always just one sentence away from contention." In the home next door, the weather might be just the opposite—"clear skies and warm temperatures with only occasional clouds and rain."

What if a reality television show were secretly broadcasting every conversation in your home? It seems from Doctrine and Covenants 1:3 that this might actually occur: "Their iniquities shall be spoken upon the housetops, and their secret acts shall be revealed." To save yourself the humiliation, try to let only good come out of your mouth. The communication patterns in a home in Bethany about A.D. 32 teach some helpful principles.

Until recently, I thought the only lesson from the biblical account of Mary and Martha was to choose things spiritual over things temporal. I've struggled to understand this brief look at Mary and Martha because Martha, the multitasker, is my kind of woman. She is the organized, keep-it-all-together, responsible sister. Martha both attended to the household needs *and* listened to the Savior. As a "Martha," I've wondered if I would get a similar response from Him. It seems a personal reprimand to me. What did Martha do to deserve the words, "Martha, Martha, thou art careful and troubled about many things: But one thing is needful: and Mary hath chosen that good part, which shall not be taken away from her"? (Luke 10:41–42).

As I have examined the account, I've decided that the Savior is actually complimenting Martha when He says she is "careful and troubled." It is good to be careful. As for troubled, isn't worry a synonym for troubled, and isn't worry a way of showing care and concern? Isn't worry what dedicated and loving wives, mothers, sisters, daughters, and friends do? Following the compliment, the Savior says that Martha lacks one thing. Just one thing! How wonderful—she's practically perfect. The only problem comes in identifying what that "needful" thing is. As I was pondering this, I thought of the possibility that the story of Mary and Martha is not only about who is careful and troubled or who sits at Jesus' feet. After reading and rereading the account, I think Mary and Martha each teach an important principle about communication in the home.

In the traditional interpretation, Martha is stressing out over meal preparation instead of seizing the opportunity to savor the Savior's words, and Mary is sitting at Jesus' feet. Then Jesus rebukes Martha and says that Mary has chosen the "better" part. The reason I put "better" in quotes is because that's what most people think the Savior said. But he didn't. Let's read Luke 10:38–42 word by word.

> Now it came to pass, as they [Jesus and his disciples] went, that he entered into a certain village: and a certain woman named Martha received him into her house. [It was Martha's house.]
>
> And she had a sister called Mary, which also sat at Jesus' feet, and heard his word. [Martha sat at Jesus' feet and heard his word. Mary is the "also."]
>
> But Martha was cumbered [burdened] about much serving, and came to him, and said, Lord, dost thou not care that my sister hath left me to serve alone? [Martha had no one to help her.] bid [tell, or perhaps, command] her therefore that she help me. [Had Martha already asked Mary to help?]

And Jesus answered and said unto her, Martha, Martha, thou art careful and troubled about many things: [I'd be stressed, too, if the Savior had come to dinner at my home.]

But one thing is needful: and Mary hath chosen that good [not *better*] part, which shall not be taken away from her. [What is "that good part"?]

Consider this. Is it possible that the reason the Savior rebuked Martha is because she found fault with her sister? One of Jesus' foremost teachings commands: "Judge not, that ye be not judged. For with what judgment ye judge, ye shall be judged: and with what measure ye mete, it shall be measured to you again" (Matt. 7:1–2). He also taught, "And why beholdest thou the mote that is in thy [sister's] eye, but considerest not the beam that is in thine own eye? Or how wilt thou say to thy [sister], Let me pull out the mote out of thine eye; and, behold, a beam is in thine own eye? Thou hypocrite, first cast out the beam out of thine own eye; and then shalt thou see clearly to cast out the mote out of thy [sister's] eye" (vv. 3–5).

Faultfinders specialize in motes, which are specks of dust. Faultfinders see the short term, the microscopic, the insignificant, the little picture. They interfere in conversations and stop the flow of life by calling attention to life's motes and by expecting others to be as interested in the myopic as they are. President Howard W. Hunter gave counsel which covers many facets, but most of the suggestions can fit under the heading, "Instead of Finding Fault . . ." This is his list:

Mend a quarrel; seek out a forgotten friend; dismiss suspicion and replace it with trust; write a letter; give a soft answer; encourage youth; manifest your loyalty in word and deed; keep a promise; forgo a grudge; forgive an enemy; apologize; try to understand; examine your demands on others; think first of someone else; be kind; be gentle; laugh a little more; express your gratitude; welcome a stranger; gladden the heart of a child; take pleasure in the beauty and wonder of the earth; speak your love and then speak it again. (*The Teachings of Howard W. Hunter,* ed. Clyde J. Williams, 271)

Faultfinding is hypocritical. A hypocrite, in part, is someone who expects more of others than he or she does of himself or herself. Hypocrites are full of pride. Martha's request was mote-finding. She said, in effect, "Mary is neglecting her duties. Mary is not helpful. Mary is using You as an excuse not to help." But Martha failed to see her own beam. She was judging her sister unrighteously. Jesus commands that you and I refrain from fault-finding, but He knows judgments must be made. "Judge not according to the appearance, but judge righteous judgment" (John 7:24). Righteous judgments are made through the Spirit. When Martha asked Jesus to intervene and arbitrate in a mundane house-hold matter, He addressed Martha lovingly, with just a hint of reproach in the sweet use of her name, "Martha, Martha." The lesson I learn from Martha is to refrain from finding fault. *Finding* implies looking and perhaps even seeking. I am not to look for faults, for then I will not find faults in others.

What is the lesson from Mary? Picture the setting in the small house in Bethany. Mary and Martha were entertaining Jesus. Providing for such a guest and the others who came with Him is an honor and a burden. I think the lesson from Mary is that she saw the honor in the opportunity; Martha saw the burden in the experience. It's obvious that Mary could have helped Martha, but she didn't. Whether Mary made a conscious decision not to let the needs of the moment take precedence over the opportunity of a lifetime (to sit at the feet of the Savior), or whether she was unaware of Martha's need, it doesn't matter. The major point is that Mary listened to the Savior, which is "that good part." As I listen to Jesus, I will entertain Him figuratively in my home and in my innermost core, and my communication patterns will improve.

Whenever I have opportunity to stay in others' homes, I watch for ways I can learn to communicate better. I love being in homes where family members cheerfully greet each other in the mornings and bid each other good night as they retire to bed. There are homes where parents (especially mothers) are literally at the crossroads, as

President Ezra Taft Benson taught. He said, "Take time to always be at the crossroads when your children are either coming or going—when they leave and return from school, when they leave and return from dates, when they bring friends home. Be there at the crossroads whether your children are six or sixteen" (*Come, Listen to a Prophet's Voice*, 32). I enjoy watching comings and goings in these homes. "Good-bye!" "Have a good day!" "Go in safety!" "I love you!" "Welcome home!" "How was your day?" My favorite of the fond farewells is "Be safe and do good." I feel loved in homes where courtesies are spoken routinely. "Please." "Thank you." "Excuse me." "I'm sorry." "What may I do to help?"

It's been my experience that in some homes, no matter what the question, "No!" is the first response. Then, thinking better of the negativity, the "no" is softened or excused in some way, which never repairs, only mitigates. On the other hand, one of my visits exposed me to a family where no matter what the question was, the first response was "Of course." If a qualification is needed, the condition comes after the positive. For example: "Will you take out the garbage?" is always answered, "Of course." Then, as needed, "Is it all right if I do it in ten minutes on my way to school?" And what is the answer? Of course, it's "Of course."

One of the settings for good communications is around the breakfast or dinner table. Another good place is in the car, especially if the ratio is one parent to one child. Another good communication location is family prayer. I enjoyed spending time with one particular family where family prayer began and ended each day. The person who was called on to pray first said a scripture that the rest of the family repeated. (The children were old enough now that the scripture was often chosen to coincide with need or circumstance.) After the "amen," they all put their arms around each other in a group hug. In another family the call to family prayer begins by either parent singing, "Let us gather in a circle," and before a minute has passed, the rest of the family has gathered to finish the song: "And kneel in family prayer, To thank our Heav'nly Father for the blessings we all share" ("Family Prayer," *Children's Songbook*, 189).

Now, this may not be your family's style, but the principle behind these actions is the key. Communication in the home is a subject of critical importance. My goal is to reach the summit suggested by Will Rogers: "Live that you wouldn't be ashamed to sell the family parrot to the town gossip."

DISCIPLINE: ARE YOU A TWO-MARSHMALLOW PERSON?

In *Emotional Intelligence,* Daniel Goleman writes about a controlled experiment done on four-year-olds to measure their ability to delay gratification. The experimenter explained to a four-year-old that if he could wait until the experimenter ran a quick errand, he could have two marshmallows as a treat. If the child could not wait, he could have only one, but he could have it right then. Ever since I read of this experiment and the results, I've become more aware of my own self-gratification tendencies, and I have observed how, as Goleman puts it, the "eternal battle between impulse and restraint . . . desire and self-control, gratification and delay"(79) plays out. Dr. Goleman says that the psychological skill to resist impulse is the foundation of all others.

In the study, the experimenter would be gone for fifteen to twenty minutes, leaving the child alone. Some children grabbed their one marshmallow immediately. Some waited. Through two-way mirrors, the experimenters watched the children who were delaying gratification. "To sustain themselves in their struggle they covered their eyes so they wouldn't have to stare at temptation, or rested their heads in their arms, talked to themselves, sang, played games with their hands and feet, even tried to go to sleep" (ibid., 80).

When these children reached adolescence, they were tracked and reevaluated. The children who had resisted the quick marshmallow at age four stayed that way: "Those who had resisted temptation at four were now, as adolescents, more socially competent, personally effective, self-assertive, and better able to cope with the frustrations of life. . . . They were self-reliant and confident, trustworthy and dependable; and they took initiative and plunged into projects. And, they were still able to delay gratification in pursuit of their goals." On the other hand, the one-marshmallow adolescents were "more likely to . . . shy away from social contacts, be stubborn and indecisive, easily upset by frustrations, to think of themselves as *bad* or unworthy . . . and they were still, after all those years, unable to put off gratification" (ibid., 80).

The most amazing statistic came, however, when these same children were reevaluated in their senior year in high school. "Those who had waited patiently at four were far superior as students to those who had acted on whim. . . . Most astonishingly, they had dramatically higher scores on their SAT tests. The third of children who at four grabbed for the marshmallow most eagerly had an average verbal score of 524 and math score of 528; the third who waited longest had average scores of 610 and 652—a difference of 210 points in total score" (*ibid,* 81).

Discipline defined is the ability to delay gratification, and this trait seems to be the core essence of true success. Is there anything more important to an individual and to society than self-discipline? A person with self-discipline can turn away from temptation and can expend the effort necessary to work hard and find ways to achieve goals. Can self-discipline be taught to our children? Yes, indeed. And the first way is, of course, to learn self-discipline ourselves. The second part in the equation in raising self-disciplined children is that the disciplining is fair—a blend of mercy and justice—consistent, and boringly predictable. Some parents maintain that discipline stifles children and is abusive, but when I learned that the root of the word *discipline* is *disciple,* then everything I thought about the value of discipline was reinforced. Is there anything more important for a member of The Church of Jesus Christ of Latter-day Saints than to work toward being a disciple—*a believer and follower of Christ?* It seems to work this way: a mother disciplines herself to become more like Jesus Christ, and in the process disciplines her child in a Christlike way, which results in a child who learns to discipline himself.

President Spencer W. Kimball said the following about discipline:

> The term may not be popular in this age of license and
> lack of restraint, but what is needed is self-discipline.

Can we imagine the angels or the gods not being in control of themselves in any particular? The question is of course ludicrous. Equally ridiculous is the idea that any of us can rise to the eternal heights without disciplining ourselves and being disciplined by the circumstances of life. The purity and perfection we seek is unattainable without this subjection of unworthy, ungodlike urges and the corresponding encouragement of their opposites. We certainly cannot expect the rules to be easier for us than for the Son of God, of whom it is recorded: *"Though he were a Son, yet learned he obedience by the things which he suffered"* (Heb. 5:8; emphais in original). . . . Repentance . . . is the way to annul the effects of a previous lack of obedience [discipline] in one's life." (*The Miracle of Forgiveness*, 28)

In my experience, I've found that most of the time children know when they have done something wrong and expect, want, to be disciplined. Though they will deny it, experiencing the consequences of their behavior actually helps them feel better about themselves. Sometimes I gave a child a second chance, just to have the child repeat the misbehavior. But when I enforced an appropriate punishment, the child seemed to respond by accepting the punishment and not repeating the deed. Sometimes I have unintentionally hurt a child by not disciplining him because I thought mercy should override justice. As an older mother, I let justice do its job. Disciplining a child says "I care about you" and "I love you." Sure, some children will make you feel guilty about the discipline you *invoke*, but you aren't campaigning for their votes. Motherhood isn't a popularity contest. When a child knows that his parents are prayerful, when he knows they are motivated by love, when he knows they are consistent in their beliefs, attitudes, and parenting, when he knows there are consequences if he doesn't behave in certain ways, healthy personalities emerge.

Three good disciplining techniques are:

1. **Time-out.** This is a good technique to discipline a young child, age eight and younger, who is momentarily out of control. Mother

says, in a very in-control tone, something such as, "Your actions tell me you are asking for a time-out." Even a two-year-old knows when he needs to sit on his time-out chair or go to his time-out place. (The time-out place must *not* be scary or dangerous. Time-out is discipline, not punishment.) For tantrums, teasing, and fighting, time-outs work well. Consistency is the operative word. If something deserves a time-out one day, and the behavior is repeated, there must be another time-out—perhaps a little longer this time. A small child should stay in time-out only a minute or two, just until he realizes he is being disciplined and needs to change his behavior. One mother taught her eighteen-month-old not to throw food off his high chair tray by holding both his little hands in hers and saying, "Nathan, we don't throw food." Then she would continue to hold his hands while she counted slowly to twenty. There were at least two good results. Nathan learned to hand his mother the food he didn't want on his tray, and he learned to count to twenty. An older child can stay in time-out much longer.

Another effective time-out is toy time-out. When a toy or object is being misused either to hurt someone or damage something, or when children are fighting over it, mother gives a warning, and if the behavior continues, she calmly takes the toy or object and puts it in time-out. The child cannot have it back until it will be used properly. A toy can stay in time-out for days, weeks, perhaps years. I put a set of handcuffs in toy time-out for one year after my six-year-old son, within fifteen minutes of receiving the handcuffs as a birthday gift, handcuffed his grandpa to a bed rail. My father thought that since the handcuffs were a toy, he could easily escape and therefore allowed himself to be handcuffed. It was about twenty minutes before anyone realized that grandpa was missing. I had to find the six-year-old, and he had to find the key before grandpa could be let out of his prison. It made a funny family memory, but I didn't find it amusing at the time.

Just a few more thoughts about time-outs. There should be *no* interaction during time-out. Just go on about your work. Discipline yourself not to verbally reprimand the child during time-out. Never be brought into a negotiating scenario with the child who tries to bargain for an early end to the time-out. The time starts counting when the child is calm. As mentioned, time-outs work best for children ages eight and under.

For older children, withholding privileges is a technique that works about the same way. Just a word or two about withholding privilege as a form of punishment: again, like time-out, it can become abusive. Even if not abusive, the punishment must fit the crime. For example, an eighth grader got a C+ in an English class I taught. He did the work, but English was not his favorite subject, nor did he have the aptitude necessary to get the A his mother wanted him to get. He wrote me a letter that explained that when he'd brought the report card home, his mother became angry and told him that he wasn't putting in enough time and could not play on the community basketball team, which he loved and was good at, until he brought up his English grade. By the time he could bring up the grade, next report-card time, the basketball season would be over. As this boy's English teacher, I saw that he didn't work any harder or raise his grade; there was no reward for working harder. Ill-conceived punishment can harm and deflate a child's desire to be obedient and productive.

There may be times that you give yourself a time-out. Since you never want to discipline in frustration or anger, a quiet moment or two to regroup and offer up a quick but sincere prayer helps you calm down as nothing else. Many bathrooms in many homes have been used as mother's time-out place where she spends her private moments praying for help in learning appropriate ways to discipline.

2. **Positive reinforcement**. This is another way a mother molds behavior. When she observes a child approximating a desired behavior, she acknowledges him for it. When a child shares a toy or candy bar, helps without being asked, does an assigned chore in a timely way, responds politely, or makes peace, you should show approval in words, hugs, and smiles. On other occasions, let the child overhear you telling another adult about his or her good deeds. Children thrive on praise. Find ways to praise *each* child, not just those who are easy to praise and who receive a lot of it. Praise raises. But as with everything else, praise can be overdone. A child doesn't need praise for every good action. You and I do many good things because that's how we are; we need to be careful not to make praise the child's only motive for doing good.

3. **Don't interfere with consequences.** A third disciplining technique is to step back and do nothing—well, seemingly nothing. A mother who allows natural consequences of a child's actions to do the majority of the disciplining finds a most successful technique. By allowing the child to experience the consequences of his behavior—both good and bad—life's lessons are taught. If a sixteen-year-old gets a speeding ticket, he pays the ticket and the insurance increase. If a child doesn't finish a homework assignment before the family has planned to watch TV (a reward and privilege), he misses the opportunity until the homework is completed. If a child refuses to do his homework over the long-term, his grades suffer, scholarships are lost, and future schooling requires more work than it needed to.

As you discipline with natural consequences, stay calm, firm, loving, and refrain from saying, "I told you so" or, "I'm doing this for your own good." Say nothing. This is a case in which anything you say will be held against you. Natural consequences don't work with a mother's commentary going on in the background. The benefit to disciplining with natural consequences is that the child realizes that there are consequences to his or her behavior. Gradually he or she will correlate the fact that consequences to actions may be positive or negative, and that positives come from good choices and good actions.

Let natural consequences discipline when possible. Be consistent. Teach correct behavior at appropriate times. Be calm and empathetic. And when you find a disciplining technique that works with a child, use it sparingly. The tendency will be to use it often because it works. If a technique is overused, it will become less effective. These three ways to discipline bring order and predictability to the child's and mother's lives. And another wonderful thing about using these techniques is that your children will learn from your example and discipline their children, your grandchildren, the same way.

As you teach discipline, be disciplined. Resist impulses and allow your children to observe the choices you make. Share with your children why you make certain decisions and how you are patient with fulfillment. Be a two-marshmallow mother!

COUNSEL:
HOW WELL DO I TAKE IT?

I went with Terry and Michelle, my son-in-law and daughter, and their children to Walt Disney World as an extra set of eyes, ears, and hands. We were standing in line to take a safari ride when we noticed an employee talking to everyone in line. When the man got to us he said, "This safari ride travels on bumpy, rutted, dirt roads. Do any of you have back or neck problems?" I told him that I had been in a car accident and had gotten whiplash. The man said, "Please do not go on this ride." I thanked him for alerting me to the potential danger and did not go on the ride. Later, I heard Michelle using this situation as a teaching moment to remind her children how wise I was to take counsel from someone who knew the hazards of the road ahead.

I know teaching children to take counsel is very important, but I've been reminded many times in my life how important it is for me to take counsel. It was easy to take the counsel from the park employee. It's not always that easy to take counsel from others. The truth about counsel is that everyone can benefit from it. No person is too wise. All Church Presidents have counselors who counsel them. The scriptures tell us that even the Gods counsel together: "And the Gods took counsel among themselves" (Abr. 4:26).

"Counsel with the Lord in all thy doings, and he will direct thee for good" (Alma 37:37). How do I counsel with the Lord? Do I ask in prayer for His guidance and then follow it? Do I seek His counsel through His holy words in scripture, in conference talks, and through the Holy Ghost? I'd better—because my attitude toward counsel will affect my children's attitude toward counsel. When their teachers, leaders, or parents give counsel, how will it be received? When the child's future spouse, employer, bishop, or prophets give counsel, how will it be accepted? Most likely, my children will respond to counsel much like I do. A mother who listens, evaluates, appreciates, seeks, and, when wisdom indicates, acts on the counsel, exemplifies humility. Such a mother shows that counsel gives perspective and provides a valuable tool in navigating the bumpy road of life.

The Lord said to the wandering, disobedient children of Israel, "For they are a nation void of counsel, neither is there any understanding in them" (Deut. 32:28). If I refuse God's or His servants' counsel, there is no understanding in me. Proverbs states, "The way of a fool is right in his own eyes: but he that hearkeneth unto counsel is wise" (Prov. 12:15). Proverbs 19:20 reminds us, "Hear counsel, and receive instruction, that thou mayest be wise in thy latter end."

Nephi cautions that if I think I am wise, I will believe a ploy of the evil one. "O that cunning plan of the evil one! O the vainness, and the frailties, and the foolishness of men! When they are learned they think they are wise, and they hearken not unto the counsel of God, for they set it aside, supposing they know of themselves, wherefore, their wisdom is foolishness and it profiteth them not. And they shall perish" (2 Ne. 9:28).

Seek counsel from Father in Heaven in prayer. Ask for the Holy Ghost to bless you with ideas. Pray for wisdom and understanding to see things as they really are. Be aware that the evil one may offer counterfeit counsel. But there is another source of counsel that can be emphasized.

Heavenly Father uses mortals to counsel other mortals. He expects me to seek and listen to advice and warnings from persons He places in positions to influence me: family members, Church leaders and teachers, fellow sisters in the gospel, and my husband. These may be my sentinels, like the safari-ride employee, put in my path to keep me from making choices that will cause physical and spiritual harm.

Counsel from most humans doesn't come labeled as such—no neon signs or flag waving. A drum roll does not precede the advice, guidance, or warning. It is usually subtle—valuable, important, perhaps critical—not fluorescent.

I've found counsel may come:

• As the topic the bishop discusses in a combined priesthood and Relief Society lesson.

• In a subject my visiting teaching companion talks to me about seemingly in passing.

• As a double-dose of a principle, as when an *Ensign* article and a sacrament meeting talk emphasize the same point.

• When my child's schoolteacher hints at a concern.

• In words or phrases my husband uses in prayers.

• In a phrase from a verse of scripture or a hymn not noticed before.

Another issue with counsel taking is that it seems to be my nature when I receive unwanted counsel, however true I know it is, to think that somehow I am the exception, that the counsel doesn't apply to me. That's when I need to remember the truth of Ecclesiastes 1:9, which reminds me that I am *not* the exception: "There is no new thing under the sun."

Exceptions to the rules of life are very rare. An example: several years ago, President Gordon B. Hinckley gave a talk on getting out of debt. I've always known how important getting and staying out of debt is, but I didn't think to myself, when I heard the talk, "Now how does this counsel apply to me? What action or response to this prophetic counsel is necessary on my part?" About two days after the talk, I was putting gas in my car when a friend pulled up in her new SUV. I noticed a "for sale" sign in the window. "Why are you selling your lovely new car?" I asked.

She paused and thought, and then said, "We're doing the debt thing."

"The debt thing?" I asked.

"Yes," she said. "You know—President Hinckley's talk. We've decided to sell this and get a used van." A day or two later, another friend told me they had tightened their budget to pay off their home faster. I had listened. But they had taken action. I had just thought about it. I know that when I think I am an exception, it's simply an excuse. I know that as I follow good counsel, I will avoid pitfalls, and if I don't heed wise counsel, the jungle-safari ride will bump and jolt and perhaps cause injury to me. I want to avoid spiritual whiplash. I want to listen to and follow counsel from God and those He places in my path to warn me of dangers in the road ahead.

If I become figuratively deaf and blind to counsel and refuse to respond to the positive message, I allow pride a foothold in my heart. But if I not only humbly receive counsel when it is, metaphorically, set on my doorstep, but also ask for and seek it, the Lord will be able to help me be the kind of woman He needs me to be. When I view counsel as a gift from God, I will be blessed to see situations more clearly and not only hear the counsel, but act on it.

DEBT:
MAKING DOLLARS AND SENSE

Doing the debt thing," as mentioned in the essay "Counsel," started with President Hinckley's words in October 1998: "There is the portent of stormy weather ahead." His counsel to get out of debt came on the heels of one of the most prosperous periods in U.S. history. The trouble with prosperous times is that the American way seems to be to let expenses rise to the level of income and beyond. The extent of financial irresponsibility in past eras was described as living from paycheck to paycheck, but now it's maxing out numerous credit cards. The biblical account of Joseph who was sold into Egypt exemplifies fiscal wisdom. The Bible says the Egyptians prepared for the seven lean years by saving twenty percent during the years of plenty. My mother always lived by this maxim: Make four dollars, spend five dollars, live in agony. Make four dollars, spend three dollars, live in joy.

If you have debt, you know that it is a form of slavery. You also know how wonderful it would be to be debt free. Is such a goal possible? How long would it take? Consider this accelerated debt-reduction plan.

Make a list of all debts from smallest to largest. List to whom the money is owed, the minimum payment due each month, the interest rate, and the total amount due. Just for example, let's say the smallest debt is $400 to Mervyn's and the minimum monthly payment is $25. All you have to do is double that payment to $50. Then, as soon as the Mervyn's bill is paid in full, you have $50 a month to add to the next debt on your list. For example, if you owe $600 on your Visa card and the minimum due is $35, you now have that additional $50 to add to the $35, for a total monthly payment of $85. As soon as that debt is paid in full, you have $85 to put toward the next debt. The average American family can be debt free using this method, *including mortgage,* in six to nine years! (Though I have seen this method work very effectively, obviously the number of years it takes to pay off your debt with this method is contingent on your debt-to-income ratio.)

Then when the debts are all paid, what do you do with all that money? Pay yourself by saving money, pay extra fast offerings, invest, help others, and gather assets for the lean years of retirement, recession, or when your family needs are the greatest. Shift from making payments to someone else, and make them to yourself. Earn interest instead of paying interest. All the previous is explained in a booklet that is free from Church Distribution Centers. It's called *One for the Money* by Elder Marvin J. Ashton. You may also want to read President Gordon B. Hinckley's article "Climbing Out of Debt" (*Ensign,* July 2002, 67).

To illustrate the enslaving nature of debt, let's ask how long it takes to pay off a $2,400 credit-card debt if you pay the minimum monthly payment of $48? As impossible as it seems, 43.6 years! How long does it take to pay off that debt if you take advantage of the offer to skip a payment every December? Almost twice as long—85.2 years (see flagshipnews.com).

Debt truly is slavery. As President J. Reuben Clark Jr. said:

> Interest never sleeps nor sickens nor dies; it never goes to the hospital; it works on Sundays and holidays; it never takes a vacation; it never visits nor travels; it takes no pleasure; it is never laid off work nor discharged from employment; it never works on reduced hours; it never has short crops nor droughts; it never pays taxes; it buys no food; it wears no clothes; it is unhoused and without home and so has no repairs, no replacements, no shingling, plumbing, painting, or whitewashing; it has neither wife, children, father, mother, nor kinfolk to watch over and care for; it has no expense of living; it has neither weddings nor births nor deaths; it has no love, no sympathy; it is as hard and soulless

as a granite cliff. Once in debt, interest is your companion every minute of the day and night; you cannot shun it or slip away from it; you cannot dismiss it; it yields neither to entreaties, demands, or orders; and whenever you get in its way or cross its course or fail to meet its demands, it crushes you. (*Conference Report,* Apr. 1938, 101)

Remember the other side of the coin, where interest works for you. It also never sleeps. A family invested $250 in 1973 and forgot about it. Recently they discovered that this $250 account had grown to $12,000.

Lending companies, whose profits are based on the interest borrowers pay to them, offer two lures—a second mortgage and debt consolidation loans. Both are extremely risky. They are wolves in sheeps' clothing—though disguised, debt by any other name is still debt. I've heard that eighty percent of persons who get a debt consolidation loan within two years have accumulated as much new debt as when they initially sought debt consolidation. Their behavior hasn't changed; they have not learned to differentiate between needs and wants, or learned financial discipline.

Bankruptcy is not the answer. Bankruptcy has been called "a ten-year mistake" (bankruptcy.org) because it destroys your credit, among other things, like your self-esteem and self-sufficiency.

Experts suggest three priorities for wise financial planning. First, purchase a modest home and pay off the mortgage as soon as possible. Second, save ten percent of all income and more during prosperous times; and third, pay off all debt. If you are addicted to debt, try canceling credit cards and your overdraft protection, and whenever you are tempted to assume more debt, discipline yourself by enforcing a mandatory twenty-four-hour waiting period before you buy anything. If impulse buying is a problem, go shopping for necessities with only enough cash to pay for the items on your list. Leave your checkbook and credit cards at home. A compulsive online shopper quit "cold turkey" in a moment of strength and resolve by canceling her credit card.

President Hinckley said he was not prophesying calamity, but a prophet is a prophet. We can benefit by heeding his counsel. The principles of freeing oneself from the cruel taskmaster of debt are true in any economic scenario and in any income bracket. Work to be debt free, to pay yourself rather than creditors, and to earn rather than pay interest. Will Rogers is credited with saying, "The quickest way to double your money is to fold it and put it back in your pocket" (humorsource.com). It makes sense—and dollars.

A RECIPE FOR ANGER

A few years ago I wrote a script for a Relief Society presentation. The night of the performance, I was more than surprised that another sister took credit for writing it. I felt more sadness than anger, but was reminded of a story about Charles W. Penrose, who wrote the words to hymn number 336, "School Thy Feelings."

In 1869 Brother Penrose, who later became a member of the Quorum of the Twelve Apostles, was in the presidency of the mission in Birmingham, England. To furnish the office, he bought furniture with his own money. When he was released from the mission, he took his furniture home. A fellow Church member accused him of stealing Church property, which deeply hurt his feelings to the point of anger. He thought of ways to retaliate, but instead wrote:

> *School thy feelings, O my brother; Train thy warm, impulsive soul. Do not its emotions smother, But let wisdom's voice control. School thy feelings; there is power In the cool, collected mind. Passion shatters reason's tower, Makes the clearest vision blind. School thy feelings, O my brother; Train thy warm, impulsive soul. Do not its emotions smother, But let wisdom's voice control.* (see George D. Pyper, *Stories of Latter-day Saint Hymns,* 158–60)

How times have changed from 1869 to today, when anger is considered normal and even entertaining on radio and television. *Venting* is a term used to make anger seem healthy. But anger is still a dagger that hurts and scars; it's ugly and contagious. Anger is the polar opposite of love, for "where love is, there God is also" ("Where Love Is," *Children's Songbook,* 138) and where anger is, there Satan is also. To me the greatest problem with anger is the sacrifice made by those who choose anger. What is that sacrifice? As anger begins to stir the emotions and cloud reason, the Spirit of the Lord is repulsed. To me, life is hard even with the Holy Ghost as a guide. The loss of the Spirit is ruinous. Satan is the "father of contention, and he stirreth up the hearts of men to contend with *anger,* one with another" (3 Ne. 11:29; emphasis added). From the *Ensign* I found this analogy: "The verb *stir* sounds like a recipe for disaster: Put tempers on medium heat, stir in a few choice words, and bring to a boil; continue stirring until thick; cool off; let feelings chill for several days; serve cold; lots of leftovers" (Lynn G. Robbins, "Agency and Anger," May 1998, 80).

Anger short-circuits wisdom and sound judgment. Making "a decision while angry is like a captain [putting] out to sea in a raging storm. Only injury and wreckage result from wrathful moments" (ElRay L. Christiansen, "Be Slow to Anger," *Ensign*, June 1971, 37). Anger is a blade wounding the angry person, disappointing (at a minimum) those who are the targets, and causing sadness in bystanders who have to witness the human storm.

Anger is a choice. Angry people feel their anger is justified for any number of reasons, but the most common is "you (she, he, it) made me angry." In reality, that is as inaccurate as saying, "The ice cream made me fat," when you are the one who moves the spoon to your mouth. Someone or something cannot make you angry. You make you angry. The second most common excuse is "I can't help it." In actual fact, you can help getting angry. It's the same as saying, "I can't help eating ice cream." Allowing yourself to become angry is *your* choice. That's why Elder Penrose chose the word *school.* You can learn to discipline and control anger.

Anger may become a habitual way to address unpleasant surprises, or to respond to others' anger, or to react when you feel offended. You may use anger as a tool to control others. And anger feeds on anger. You may start out with one angry person and end up with a mob. The more you allow anger to lie in wait in your emotional core, the more situations will trigger anger and hijack your wisdom and common sense. Aggressive actions such as screaming, yelling, swearing, throwing things, giving the silent treatment, and name-calling are all learned strategies of expressing anger. You either express your anger in a way that has proven effective for you in the past, or you copy behaviors you have observed in others.

But since all habits are learned, anger can be unlearned. You can control your angry thoughts, your angry acting out, and your angry words, because Heavenly Father has given you a gift to overcome anger. That gift is agency, which gives you the ability to decide how you will respond in any scenario. *Agency,* defined, is "the ability and privilege God gives people to choose and to act for themselves" (*Guide to the Scriptures,* lds.org). I am going to go way out on a limb here and give an opinion about agency. Agency is often taught as the right to choose evil or good, and many scriptures point this out. I think, however, that agency is also Heavenly Father's gift to His children to choose *right.* Evil is everywhere, and Satan can use any and every devious tactic to seduce a person. He binds his prey with a flaxen thread until they bind themselves with cords of abuse or addiction. Then they are his subjects and have lost their agency. As Jesus said to the Nephites, "Watch and pray always lest ye enter into temptation; for Satan desireth to have you, that he may sift you as wheat" (3 Ne. 18:18). This is your value to Satan.

To Heavenly Father, you are a precious child with the potential to become as He is. His purpose, work, and glory are to give you immortality and eternal life. The Apostle Paul wrote, "Eye hath not seen, nor ear heard, neither have entered into the heart of man, the things which God hath prepared for them that love him" (1 Cor. 2:9). What are you to Satan? No more than a grain of wheat to sift. What does he promise you? Nothing, only to be as miserable as he is. Unless I actively and continuously choose good, I will lose the priceless gift of agency, or at least make it much harder to use. That's why anger must be appreciated for what it is—a tool of the adversary.

Anger is dangerous in that it can limit your self-control if not checked immediately. One morning a friend called me and briefly described a situation which didn't make a lot of sense. As I learned later, she was leaving out essential information. Anyway, her voice was somewhere between sobbing and yelling. She asked me what she could do to control the anger she was feeling. I said, "How angry are you? Are you mad, angry, or feeling rage?"

"How do you define rage?" she asked.

"Rage is anger intensified to violence," I said, praying to receive help for her and for me.

"I just called my husband's boss and yelled at him," she confessed. "I have never felt like this before in my entire life. I am out of control."

So we talked and talked until she felt she could deal with the situation. A month or so later, she thanked me for helping her that morning and said, "I never want to get that angry again. My emotions and body seemed separate from my brain. I can see how I could actually do physical harm. I scared myself. I didn't know that I could feel such emotion and act so irrationally."

Anger is stupid. The best illustration that anger is unintelligent and a complete waste of energy, emotion, and time is found in this true story. A man and his friend were golfing. Golfing to this man was serious business. At the second tee, he swung. The ball went farther than he anticipated, and he didn't see where it landed. A long string of obscenities and curses polluted the green. A golf course worker who was standing nearby saw the ball land. "Go look in the cup," he said to the angry man. The golfer couldn't see the ball because he had hit a hole in one! Imagine the embarrassment he could have saved himself by simply controlling his anger.

There are solutions. Anger management classes and/or professional help may be needed to resolve anger tendencies, but it can't hurt to try simpler solutions before seeking professional help. Remember that anger feeds on itself and that as the anger builds, passion and force escalate, so lessons learned from experience and wisdom dissipate. To conquer anger, you will need to marshal all the desire, discipline, determination, and prayer available so you can halt the rise of anger and not lose the help of the Holy Ghost. The most effective way of curtailing an episode of anger is to stop angry feelings at their first intimations. The first few sparks are when a few sprinkles of water can douse the fire. If the anger is left to feed on itself, it may take a figurative hook-and-ladder truck to extinguish the blaze. Perhaps some of the following ideas may also help:

Start speaking in a softer, gentler voice. President David O. McKay said, "Let husband and wife never speak in loud tones to each other, unless the house is on fire" (*Stepping Stones to an Abundant Life,* 294). President Gordon B. Hinckley said, "Lower [your] voices a few decibels" ("Each a Better Person," *Ensign,* Nov. 2002, 99).

Realize that your anger is causing bitterness and discouragement. "[Wives], love your [husbands], and be not bitter against them," and "[Mothers,] provoke not your children to anger, lest they be discouraged" (Col. 3:19, 21).

Try smiling. President Hinckley said: "We can smile when anger might be so much easier. We can exercise self-control and self-discipline and dismiss any affront levied against us" ("Each a Better Person," *Ensign,* Nov. 2002, 99).

Ask for a hug. Dr. Laura Schlessinger recently received a call on her radio talk show from a woman who often became angry at her husband and children. Dr. Laura suggested a plan. Paraphrased, it went something like this: "The next time you begin to feel anger, stop the anger midstream and ask someone to give you a hug. Try it for a few days and report back." When the woman called back, she told about the first time she tried using a hug to neutralize anger. She said she was playing with her three young children and tending her hyperactive nephew when she started getting angry. She said she decided to try Dr. Laura's suggestion and said to her eight-year-old son, "Mama needs a hug." The request took the child by surprise. He hesitated. The mother said that fear struck her as she realized that he might refuse. Then he ran to her. She said her anger dissolved as she hugged him back! The woman went on to tell how another time she called a friend for a telephone hug. Again the anger was defused.

Remove yourself from the situation. If you can't physically remove yourself, go somewhere in your brain. Divert your attention to something positive, sweet, happy, or even neutral.

Identify what triggers your anger. Refuse to be detonated by external or internal triggers. Even a bomb can't explode without something to ignite it. Pay attention to what triggers your anger, and watch for it so you are more self-aware when it comes.

Talk it through. From the talk quoted earlier, Elder ElRay L. Christiansen gave this little rhyme:

A little explained, a little endured,
A little passed over, and the quarrel is cured.

Remember the words of Jesus Christ. "Behold, this is not my doctrine, to stir up the hearts of [women] with anger, one against another; but this is my doctrine, that such things should be done away" (3 Ne. 11:30). Anger is *not* His way!

Ridding your heart and soul of anger is a gift you can give to those closest to you. As you find ways to control anger, you will be rewarded abundantly. You will receive more of that most desirable of all gifts, the active influence of the Holy Ghost in your life. As you control your anger, you will trade Satan's influence for God's influence. Could there be a better gift to give or receive?

ADVERSITY

The night before my scheduled shoulder surgery, with my right arm hanging limp at my side, my husband and son-in-law gave me a blessing. The surgeon had guaranteed the operation would relieve the pain 100 percent, but he gave only a 50 percent chance that I would ever regain full use of my arm. The blessing, on the other hand, promised a complete recovery, including the words "full range of motion."

Nearly five months passed during which I went to therapy two or three days a week and did the prescribed exercises at home on the other days. No matter how hard I tried, I could only move my arm just above shoulder height, 180 degrees. I desperately needed the full 360-degree range. I was confused. Perhaps the blessing had meant that 180-degree range of motion with no pain *was* a complete recovery; perhaps I just had to keep doing the exercises; perhaps my full recovery would come in the Resurrection. Without more range of motion and strength, I couldn't vacuum; clean a mirror; comb my hair; get dressed if there were buttons, snaps, or zippers in the back; play the piano; or carry a gallon of milk or a grandbaby.

Three days before Thanksgiving, I was with one of my daughters in a warehouse store. I turned a corner and fell over a forklift someone had left in the aisle, injuring my ankle. It was extremely painful. The X ray showed no broken bones, but the ankle was badly sprained. The doctor wrapped my ankle and sent me home with painkillers and crutches. As I was wheeled to the car in a wheelchair, I wondered how I could possibly prepare Thanksgiving dinner for twenty with a weak, immobile shoulder *and* a sprained ankle.

When we got home, my daughter brought the crutches to me so that I could get into the house. When I tried to put the crutch under my bad shoulder, the pain was excruciating. My shoulder was so weak that I could not use the crutches. The only way I could get upstairs and into the house was to crawl. Crawling hurt my shoulder (and my knees), but that pain was insignificant compared to the pain I felt when I tried to use the crutches. With much help I got through Thanksgiving, crawling almost everywhere around the house. The first few days I slumped along like a wounded puppy, but as the days went on, I could crawl faster, and the shoulder pain was almost gone.

In about ten days my ankle was well enough that I could hobble instead of crawl, and at some point, I realized that my right shoulder didn't hurt when I used the crutch. I raised my arm to see how high it would go. To my total amazement, it was better—completely and absolutely better—with 360 degrees of motion plus the strength to lift that gallon of milk and carry sweet grandbabies. I chided myself for the negative thoughts and murmuring I had done. I had thought the sprained ankle was the adversity wolf at my door, adding the adversity of a sprained ankle to the adversity of an immobile shoulder, when in actuality, it was the miracle needed to heal my shoulder as the blessing had promised.

No one wants to be an expert on adversity, but since the adversity wolf knows my address, I've observed some of his tactics. I've found he's always out to get you. When you don't have enough money, he comes in the form of discouragement; when you have plenty of money, he comes in the form of pride; when you plant a garden, he comes as cutworms in your tomatoes; when you don't plant a garden, tomato prices skyrocket; when you finally almost get out of debt, the roof begins to leak and the water heater quits; just when you begin to understand and love your neighbor, another relationship becomes strained. Adversity also comes knocking in truly vexatious forms— earthquake, plane crash, heart attack, divorce, war. And the wolf's sense of timing is most inopportune. It seems he likes to pile on the adversity. Then just when you think you've figured out how to cope with your share of adversity in your own life, he comes to you secondhand by visiting those you love—your spouse, children, and grandchildren.

The truth is that the adversity wolf knows everyone's address. And just so you know that I have done my research, I have surveyed everyone I have ever met. One hundred percent of those polled know the adversity wolf personally. But as with the sprained ankle, adversity brings blessings, not just curses.

Lehi was well acquainted with affliction. In his last recorded words, he said to his son Jacob, "There is an opposition in all things" (2 Ne. 2:11). Benjamin Franklin's encounters with adversity taught him, "Those things that hurt, instruct. It is for this reason that wise people learn not to dread but welcome problems" (quoted in "On Being Worthy," *Ensign,* May 1989, 20). Joseph Smith's experience with adversity is expressed in his eloquent analogy: "I am like a huge, rough stone rolling down from a high mountain; and the only polishing I get is when some corner gets rubbed off by coming in contact with something else, striking with accelerated force. . . . All hell knocking off a corner here and a corner there" ("Discourse to Saints," May 1843, *DHC* 5:401).

A mother had a son who showed interest in lapidary. For Christmas she bought him a rock polisher, which resembled a little washing machine. The day after Christmas they got a rock and began to read the instructions on how to turn it into a polished stone. They put the rock in the machine and turned it on. Just as you might imagine, it made a grating, grinding, abrasive noise. "How long does this take?" the mother asked, wondering how long she could stand the noise. Her son kept reading the instructions. "It says it takes about a month," he said.

A month? It takes a month to polish one stone! How much adversity does it take to polish a person? Longer than a month. Joseph Smith used future tense when describing his polishing: "Thus I *will become* a smooth and polished shaft in the quiver of the Almighty" (*Teachings of the Prophet Joseph Smith,* 304; emphasis added).

Adversity can provide the equivalent of a Ph.D. in the graduate school of life experiences. But more than anything else, adversity clearly defines your character by revealing what you truly value. You may hope and believe that you are a courageous person, but until you meet the adversity of fear, you don't know how you will respond—cowardly or courageously. You can give lip service to the principle of turning the other cheek. But until you meet the adversity of being offended or hurt, you don't know whether you will turn the other cheek or rationalize your way into retaliating. How will the adversities of ill health, financial reverse, death, accident, or disability affect you? Will you shrink, cower, or stand boldly for the right? Will you take the adversity by the tail and use the occasion to dig deep down for the finest within you? Adversity lets you find out.

Ogden Nash's heroine, Isabel, sets an example.

> Isabel met an enormous bear,
> Isabel, Isabel, didn't care
> The bear was hungry, the bear was ravenous,
> The bear's big mouth was cruel and cavernous.
> The bear said, Isabel, glad to meet you,
> How do Isabel, now I'll eat you!
> Isabel, Isabel, didn't worry,
> Isabel didn't scream or scurry.
> She washed her hands and she straightened her hair up,
> Then Isabel quietly ate the bear up.

Isabel follows the same pattern when she meets the adversity of a wicked old witch and a hideous giant. Then she meets a troublesome doctor:

> He punched and he poked till he really shocked her.
> The doctor's talk was of coughs and chills,
> And the doctor's satchel bulged with pills.
> The doctor said unto Isabel,
> Swallow this, it will make you well.
> Isabel, Isabel, didn't worry,
> Isabel didn't scream or scurry,
> She took those pills from the pill concocter,
> And Isabel calmly cured the doctor.
> (*The Adventures of Isabel,* 1991)

Mr. Nash uses a ravenous bear, a wicked old witch, a horrid hairy giant, and a troublesome doctor to symbolize life's adversities. He uses

Isabel to symbolize coping skills. She didn't worry, didn't scream, didn't scurry, felt no rage or rancor. She washed her hands, straightened her hair, took time to eat, was self-reliant. Then she took action and dealt with the adversity. That's the key!

In the midst of trials, it's easy to feel too much emotion to see the benefits of adversity at work—changing, bettering, teaching, molding, refining, grinding, and grating in its wake. It's only as the dust of adversity is settling, when you've crawled across the iceberg, swum the swamp, or unearthed an oasis, that you look back and marvel. You marvel in God's mysterious and wondrous ways and thankfully acknowledge His omnipotent hand in your life. Faith, then, is the by-product of adversity, faith in Heavenly Father's divine plan, and faith in one's self as a survivor.

Like Isabel you can take on each adversity with finesse and decisiveness, whether it's a frozen shoulder or a hideous giant. You can practice not scurrying, screaming, and worrying. You can watch with patience to see the blessing in the sprained ankle and know that Heavenly Father's actual, true, undeniable purpose is to arm you with a survivor's faith to endure again, to fortify you with a survivor's courage to stand up boldly, and to protect you with a survivor's knowledge that through the waiting and the wading, opposition brings blessings. Then when the next adversity wolf knocks at your door, I hope you will, in faith, not scream or scurry, but wash your hands and straighten your hair and then stand ready to welcome what Heavenly Father's polishing machine can make of you.

STRESS: HOW TO
PRODUCE IT AND REDUCE IT

If I have the physiology of stress and the anatomy of the body correct, I understand that sitting atop each kidney is the adrenal gland, which secretes cortisol (adrenaline) to enable your body to react immediately to danger—the fight-or-flight response. It's this cortisol that strengthens muscles, expands lung capacity, and causes eyes to dilate, helping you run faster and see better than the bear that is chasing you. This infusion makes possible a quick and decisive response to prevent accident and save life and limb.

As wonderful as this system is, the adrenal gland can't tell the difference between a real or perceived—physical or emotional—threat. When an angry bear is charging you, you use the rush of adrenaline in the physical act of trying to escape the jaws and claws. When the threat is not physical, however, as is often the case in our modern world, you still get the rush of adrenaline but won't use it in physical activity. Consequently, it builds up and, at best, can sap energy, leaving an anxious, unsettled feeling; or, at worst, may damage the immune system, speed up aging, block healing, cause weight loss or gain, and trigger the onset or flare-up of any number of chronic illnesses.

Since bad things, stress-producing events—the jaws and claws of life—happen daily, women (especially women) frequently have rushes from the adrenal gland that are not spent in physically outmaneuvering the actual threat. An adrenaline-overloaded body expresses itself in both healthy and unhealthy ways. How do you deal with the workload, the messes, the misunderstandings, the tight finances, the disappointments, the dented fenders, the chronic or acute illnesses, the dizzy cycle that causes sleep deprivation, the stress of babies, teens, and aging parents, the weight of sin, and the grief of death? As the events of life mingle and intermingle throughout your psyche, do your coping methods cause even more stress than whatever caused the stress in the beginning, resulting in stress piled on stress? There are normal emotions, and then there are stress-producing emotions. For example, sorrow is a normal emotion; its stress-producing counterpart is despair. You see the same difference in the normal emotion of disappointment and the disquieting feeling of hostility, which is a more chronic state. Think about feeling remorse compared to withdrawal, feeling troubled compared to feeling helpless.

In researching, I found this statement:

> [It is] crucial to understand . . . why it is that sustained high levels of cortisol produced by an over-geared stress response can lead to homeostatic imbalance. This in turn affects the levels of crucial neurotransmitters in the brain such as serotonin. It is here that the connection between stress and depression becomes clearer. As . . . noted earlier, one of the behavioral consequences of the stress hormones is a heightened sense of awareness: hearing, smell, memory, all are working overtime. Short-term that's fine, but long-term it has severe neurological and psychological consequences. A little like having one's foot on the accelerator and the brake at the same time. (abc.net.au)

If a woman gives in to these stress-producing emotions, she loses her ability to feel peace and serenity, passion and excitement, meaningfulness, esteem, independence, the ability to nurture and support others, and to enjoy the process, which could be called Holy Ghost–producing emotions. The world preaches cures for stress— everything from pills to self-indulgence. But if you search the scriptures, one seemingly simple solution emerges. It's the opposite of the world's placebos. It's the opposite of how the children of Israel reacted to forty years of desert wandering. It's the opposite of fear. It's 180 degrees from how Laman and Lemuel responded to stress. The Lord's way is to look for the hopeful, to see the glimpse of blue through the storm clouds, to watch the effectual parting of the Red Sea, to go forward with faith in Jesus Christ, and to evidence it by the words you say because they reflect the thoughts you think. The children of Israel complained about everything. Laman and Lemuel murmured about everything. Complaining and murmuring are a self-fulfilling prophecy; a complaining and murmuring tongue is attached to an ungrateful heart.

Next time you meet a figurative bear face-to-face and feel the anxious nervousness that indicates an adrenaline surge, stop. Realize what is happening. You are feeling stressed. Say nothing. Pause. Give yourself a chance to combat the urge to murmur or complain. And try this: put the word *STRESSED* in capital boldface letters in your brain. Now disarm your stress by removing the *STR* and replacing it with *BL*. There you have it—*B L E S S E D   N O T   S T R E S S E D!*

You may find this strange, but when I count blessings instead of enumerating stressings, I find relief. Not that it is easy to do. I have to exert tremendous willpower and focus to think of even one blessing in my stressed-out moments. But when I've been able to do it, I've found an escape from the cauldron of all those stress-producing emotions. As I begin to replace nervous, stressful feelings with feelings of gratitude, I can actually feel the tension lessening. The tautness in my facial muscles eases; I feel I can breathe deeper. It seems my lungs expand and my brain clears. The physical as well as the emotional changes are real. The fruits of replacing stress with gratitude are the emotions the Holy Ghost provides, the greatest of which is the ability to enjoy the process despite whatever problems assail you. An "attitude of gratitude" changes lives. Gratitude is very important. It is one, actually the first, of President Hinckley's six *B*'s.

Consider this comparative analogy: There were two buckets sitting on the edge of a well. One turned to the other with mouth drooping down and said, "All I do is go down and come up and go down and come up all day long. No matter how many times I go down and come up, I always go down empty." The other little bucket smiled and said, "That's funny. My life is just like yours. All I do is go down and come up and go down and come up all day long. But no matter how many times I go down and come up, I always come up full."

This story reminds me of a day of total frustration I experienced when I thought I was going down empty. I was racing to get some errands done, darting here and there with a trail of children behind me. Finally I realized I had to go home without finishing all the errands. In my stressed state, I got on an elevator on the ground floor thinking I needed to go down to the ground floor. I looked up at the numbers to see what floor I was on. Another woman on the elevator, seeing my confusion asked, "Are you going up?"

"No," I answered, "down."

She thought perhaps she was confused and looked up to see what floor we were on. "No you aren't," she said. "You are as down as you can get!"

The great thing about that experience is that I was really on my way up, just like the little bucket. I just didn't know it. When you're worried and you can't sleep, count blessings. It's a natural elevator. You may think the "blessed not stressed" idea is a little cheesy, but it honestly works. Express gratitude to Heavenly Father in your prayers; show Him your gratitude by disciplining your thoughts and tongue. Murmur not. Feel blessed instead of stressed. Chase out the negative, and, like the little bucket, you will come up full.

SUMMERTIME

No matter how well things were going at home during the school year, the advent of summer often brought a sense of panic to my heart. How—when every ounce of energy, time, patience, intelligence, emotion, and spirituality was being drained out of me on a daily basis—could I survive the summer when the children would be at home full time? I've found some mothers never have this problem because they don't let their children stay at home during the summers. They arrange activities for them outside the home, such as sending them to camp after camp, on one extreme, or just letting them play with friends or video games from dawn to dusk, on the other extreme. The best summers are a combination of lessons or camps, free time, and family time. Over the years the following ideas helped me get through the summers. Hopefully, some of the ideas will stimulate your own thoughts for what will work with this season of the year and the season of life you are in right now.

Work together. I've found that a key to enjoying a productive summer with school-aged children is to organize them to help with housecleaning, yard work, meal preparation and cleanup, and to care for younger children. I'd like to reinforce the responsibility each child has to be a good steward over his or her own possessions. All of this contributes to the overall order of the home. "House Rules," by an anonymous author, says it well. "If you sleep on it—make it up. If you wear it—hang it up. If you drop it—pick it up. If you eat out of it—wash it. If you open it—close it. If you turn it on—turn it off. If you empty it—fill it up. If it rings—answer it. If it howls—feed it. If it cries—love it!"

Some mothers have told me that starting the day off well sets the tone for a good day. One family has a ticket that must be completed before coming to breakfast. The ticket has four age-appropriate tasks. The eight-year-old's ticket lists "say prayers, make bed, get dressed, tidy room." Another family starts the day with scripture reading and a good breakfast, then separates to do morning chores. The summer is the best time to teach yard work and the joys of gardening and home-making skills to both boys and girls. It's the best time to work on projects together such as painting the shed and reorganizing drawers, closets, and the food-storage room. Summer is also the best time to teach service. Growing vegetables and sharing the harvest is a good long-term summer service project.

Learn together. There are as many ways to learn together as there are families. One summer, I realized I couldn't help every child one-on-one as much as I wanted to. So I coined the phrase "learning stations." As I explained to the children, a learning station occurs when an older child spends time helping a younger child learn the alphabet, multiplication facts, names of states, or when children read, draw, and do puzzles together. I made the older children tutors to the younger children. I had them work together five days a week for about an hour each time. I mixed up who worked with whom. One of my sisters used an alphabet theme to organize their summer's learning. On "A days" they would eat foods that begin with A, study A animals, and learn about states that begin with A. A weekly field trip was planned to a place that began with one of the alphabet letters studied during the week. She invited me to follow the same program. My children and their cousins still talk about the "alphabet" summers they enjoyed together. Another family spent a summer learning about ancestors. Their field trips were to places the family used to live. If those places were far away, they went via the Internet. They studied historic events that happened during the ancestor's lifetime.

Some families plan a weekly library trip and read books aloud together. I recall my mother weeping as she read a passage describing Mary's blindness in Laura Ingalls Wilder's *Little House* series. She or my father also read *The Burgess Bedtime* series to us. Some of our children's favorites were *The Indian in the Cupboard* books, the

Childcraft (Field Enterprises) volume titled *Great Men and Famous Deeds,* and another Childcraft volume, *How Things Change.* We read adventure stories, Bible and Book of Mormon stories, and classics suited to the ages of the children. One of the best sources of good books, which serves also as a confirmation of how important being a reading mom is, came for me when I read *The Read-Aloud Handbook* by Jim Trelease. In the preface he quotes the Gillian Strickland poem:

> *You may have tangible wealth untold;*
> *Caskets of jewels and coffers of gold.*
> *Richer than I you can never be—*
> *I had a mother who read to me.*

In chapter three Mr. Trelease wrote, "The mother's heart is the child's classroom." To prove that statement, he gives the results of a study by Hart and Risley. For this study, thousands of hours were spent inside functioning families, tabulating the words said and sentence patterns that were used in the homes. "When the daily number of words for each group of children was projected across four years, the four-year-old child from the professional family will have heard 45 million words, the working-class child 26 million, and the welfare child only 13 million. All three children will show up for kindergarten on the same day, but one will have heard 32 million fewer words—which is a gigantic difference" (an online excerpt from the report is available at *The Early Catastrophe* [aft.org/American_educator/spring2003 /catastrophe]). For more about Jim Trelease and to read excerpts of *The Read-Aloud Handbook,* go to trelease-on-reading.com.

One mother felt one of the most important opportunities of the summer was to teach her children to be more independent. She accomplished this by declaring a "quiet time" each afternoon. Each child was to spend the time alone—no friends, no TV, no video games, no music. Appropriate activities were resting, reading, writing, scrapbooking, doing puzzles or workbooks, or completing projects such as crocheting, sketching, painting by number, or organizing a drawer. Each child had to organize and plan his or her own activities.

Play together. Too many of today's children participate only in two activities—television and video games. These are primarily individual activities. Introducing children to group activities will make playing together more memorable. Playing water-balloon volleyball, taking a weekly field trip or a vacation, camping in the backyard, playing backyard baseball and other sports, and playing board games are good family activities. One family spent the summer learning and playing old-fashioned games such as charades, dodge ball, drop the handkerchief, duck duck goose, farmer in the dell, frozen tag, Mother May I?, hopscotch, jacks, jump rope, kick the can, leapfrog, London Bridge, marbles, musical chairs, Red Rover, Simon Says, and Up Jenkins. The best thing about these games is that any supplies needed are most likely already in your home.

A favorite old-fashioned game at our house is rock school. The only two things needed are a small rock and a flight of stairs. The children sit on the bottom step, which is termed kindergarten. Mother has the rock and puts it in one of her hands while her hands are behind her back. Then she brings her fists from behind her back and puts them in front of the first child. The child then touches the hand he thinks contains the rock. Mother opens that hand. If the child guesses correctly, he moves up a step to first grade. The game continues until the first child reaches the top stair. You can use this game to teach an understanding of the laws of probability and chance.

Another game we like for teens and adults is called four papers. Every person is given four (or whatever number you decide on) slips of paper and a pen or pencil. Each person writes something on each paper. It can be anything—a line from a movie, book, or scripture, a word, a name, a title of anything—literally anything. The slips of paper are collected and put in a container, and the group is divided into teams. Play commences when one person in the first group pulls a slip of paper from the container and tries to get his team to say what's on the paper in one minute. The two rules for this round are that the person giving the clues can't use any form of the clue word(s) on the paper and there is no gesturing. Play rotates until all the papers are used up. The papers are put back into the container for the next round. In the second round the clue is limited to two words and the rules are the same. The third round is only gestures. It's really fun!

Grow together. As you and your children work, learn, and play together, you will grow closer, sibling to sibling, children to parents, and parent to child. Although the tendency is to fragment the family during the summer by keeping children going here and there for lessons and camps, you may want to rethink and stay home as a family a little more often. It may be harder on the mother initially, but it will be much more rewarding in the end. And you won't spend the whole summer in the car—dropping off here and picking up there. Not only will bonds of love be strengthened, but also such skills as creativity and cooperation will be enhanced. The children will become comrades and will know that family and home can be fun. Try some of these ideas this coming summer.

A friend who read the mother-education version of my original "Summertime" essay sent me an e-mail:

> The word "superwoman" never described me. But on the last day of school I would say to my kids, "The teachers have had you all year, but NOW YOU'RE MINE!" We read together (Newbery and Caldecott award books), went to museums, made play dough and finger paints and used them, did lots of art projects (I copied school ideas such as construction-paper mosaics), and had "family Olympics" at local parks. All my kids are now grown, and most have thanked me for those summers together. In their memories, those times have been glorified into something even *better* than they actually were!

In all of the above, know that you aren't in this alone. Rely on the Holy Ghost. He will help you smile more, hug more, organize more, and listen more. It is through His promptings and your follow-through that summers truly will be a time of working, learning, playing, and growing together.

ESTEEM:
SELF OR OTHERWISE

Did you know there is a National Association of Self-Esteem and that they have a website (self-esteem-nase.org)? At the site you can find motivational quotes and take a test to determine your self-esteem level. You can also read an essay by Robert Reasoner, "The True Meaning of Self-Esteem." I read it, and with his permission, use the following. Dr. Reasoner says a person with high self-esteem has tolerance and respect for others. He says they "accept responsibility for their actions, have integrity, take pride in their accomplishments, . . . are self-motivated, willing to take risks, capable of handling criticism, loving and lovable, seek the challenge and stimulation of worthwhile and demanding goals, and take command and control of their lives. . . . People who have healthy or authentic self-esteem . . . trust their own being to be life affirming, constructive, responsible and trustworthy" (self-esteem-nase.org). All sounds good, right?

He continues by saying that self-esteem is much more than just "feeling good," yet not in any way connected with "egotism, arrogance, conceit, narcissism [self-absorption], [or] a sense of superiority." He says those negative characteristics are actually the tools used by people with low self-esteem as defensive mechanisms, which he calls "pseudo self-esteem." "Individuals with defensive or low self-esteem typically focus on trying to prove themselves or impress others. They tend to use others for their own gain. Some act with arrogance and contempt toward others. They generally lack confidence in themselves, often have doubts about their worth and acceptability, and hence are reluctant to take risks or expose themselves to failure. They frequently blame others for their shortcomings rather than take responsibility for their actions." In studies, Dr. Reasoner reports, there is a close relationship between "low self-esteem and such problems as violence, alcoholism, drug abuse, eating disorders, school dropouts, teenage pregnancy, suicide, and low academic achievement." He states the disclaimer, however, that "it has been difficult to isolate [low self-esteem] as a primary cause using traditional experimental research methods, for it is usually only one of several contributing factors." According to Dr. Reasoner it is impossible to have too much "true" self-esteem. He thinks that is like saying a person has too much good health. "However," he admits, "it is certainly possible for individuals to have an over-inflated sense of either worth or competence"(self-esteem-nase.org).

I'd like to add a few more thoughts about self-esteem. It has been my experience that individuals with low self-esteem occupy an unfair share of others' time and energy because they are absorbers and consumers, taking from those with healthy self-esteem who know their worth and can forget themselves. True self-esteem is evidenced by the ability to self-correct and self-credit. The person who has healthy self-esteem makes the world a better place by giving more and taking less from the cumulative whole.

As another measure of self-esteem, ask yourself the following questions. This will give you ideas of areas in which you might want to improve:

Do you see life as it really is? Do you live in reality?
Do you take responsibility and do right for right reasons?
Do you know that doing good makes you feel good?
Do you strive to unlock your own and others' potential?
Do you meet life's challenges with confidence?
Do you bounce back from disappointment and failure?
Do you make a positive difference in others' lives?
Do you repent quickly and forgive easily?

Self-esteem, especially in children, is built as the child sees, as reflected in the faces of adults he trusts, that he is appreciated—held in esteem. You've heard the following riddle. Two coal miners come out of a mine after their shift. One miner has a clean face; the other has a dirty face. After they say good-bye to each other, the one with the dirty face heads straight for his car and goes home. The one with the clean face stops to wash his face before starting home. Why? The one with the clean face saw his fellow worker's dirty face and assumed his face was also dirty. The one with the dirty face saw his fellow worker's clean face and assumed his face was also clean. Similarly, what I see in your face tells me more than whether I need to wash my face. It reveals to me how much or how little I am valued.

A mother's face is her child's mirror, reflecting acceptance, rejection, irritation, approval, and on and on. The most important image a mother should reflect back to her child, as far as it is possible, is the truth about how the world really is; the closer to the truth, the better the child will become in dealing with the world. For example, a mother who compliments and praises in excess reflects unrealistic approval and creates a house of cards. A mother who condemns and chastises in excess reflects unrealistic disapproval and destroys confidence. The ideal is somewhere in between. Self-esteem is built on reality.

I feel that each person has four basic needs when it comes to developing self-esteem. Think of these as the four legs of a table. Each is necessary for a solid emotional foundation.

The need to feel accepted. From his earliest days a child knows if he is valued by the way the significant people in his life respect, enjoy, and love him.

The need to be competent. Self-esteem is built on fact. Everyone needs to know that they are good at something. Success in school is essential because so many years are spent there. Everyone needs to be good enough in reading, writing, and basic math. If a child functions below grade level, tutoring and extra practice at home are mandatory. Beyond the basics, a child or teen has talents and interests. Find out what they are by exposing the child to drawing, painting, sculpting, sewing, soccer, crocheting, ballet, drama, music, etc. Your child may want to do many things or concentrate on one. Don't hold the bar so high that no matter how hard she tries she can never please you or so low that he can step over it without much effort. Especially if your child struggles in school, help him or her find other activities in which he or she can excel and identify.

The feeling that he or she is good. Children need the feeling that they are good and decent. As they live up to a standard, they feel good about themselves. Children innately know what Abraham Lincoln verbalized, "When I do good, I feel good" (quotedb.com).

The feeling that one has power. As children are given responsibility, as they are allowed to make choices, as they influence and make a difference in their environment, they gain confidence and self-esteem. Children need to be accountable—take appropriate credit for good actions and appropriate blame for inappropriate actions. Children who can meet life's challenges face-to-face and surmount obstacles can do so because they know they are accountable to themselves.

I hope all of the above is a concise and accurate treatment of self-esteem. I agree with most everything Dr. Reasoner says. In fact, I wrote a book on the subject in 1986. The complete emphasis of the book was that "every mother needed to take charge of and maintain her own self-esteem." Since I wrote those words, however, I've had some maturing experiences, and, although I still believe that building self-esteem is an important part of negotiating the trials of life, it is not the ultimate answer.

One of my "maturing experiences" came on April 1, 1996, with a breast cancer diagnosis. It's amazing what a life-threatening illness can do. Through those months of being sicker than sick and balder than bald, I learned for myself what Primary children have sung for years: "I will follow God's plan for me" (*Children's Songbook,* 164). The self-esteem movement is a world-centered answer for navigating through life. The gospel is the Christ-centered answer to help you plot a course to eternal life. It matters where you want to go. Jesus said it this way: "And this is life eternal, that they might know thee the only true God, and Jesus Christ, whom thou hast sent" (John 17:3). I think I can trace the evolution of my growth from thinking that healthy self-esteem solved all problems to where I was willing to trust

God the Father and His Son Jesus Christ to give me peace about issues I could not deal with on my own.

In December 1986, when I was still thinking self-esteem was the answer, President Ezra Taft Benson suggested that I turn myself over to God. He said: "Men and women who turn their lives over to God will discover that He can make a lot more out of their lives than they can. He will deepen their joys, expand their vision, quicken their minds, strengthen their muscles, lift their spirits, multiply their blessings, increase their opportunities, comfort their souls, raise up friends, and pour out peace. Whoever will lose his life in the service of God will find eternal life" (as quoted in *Teachings of Ezra Taft Benson,* 361). I logged his words but still didn't understand them.

During my recovery, however, I read several C. S. Lewis books. *Mere Christianity* expanded my vision as to what God will do with me if I let Him. I learned the difference between self-esteem, wherein I make my life into what I think it should be, and esteeming God's plan, which is turning my life over to God and allowing Him to make of me what He wants me to be.

C. S. Lewis wrote:

> Imagine yourself as a living house. God comes in to rebuild that house. At first, perhaps, you can understand what He is doing. He is getting the drains right and stopping the leaks in the roof and so on. You knew that those jobs needed doing and so you were not surprised. But presently He starts knocking the house about in a way that hurts and does not seem to make sense. What on earth is He up to? The explanation is that He is building quite a different house from the one you thought of—throwing out a new wing here, putting on an extra floor there, running up towers, making courtyards. You thought you were going to be made into a decent little cottage; but He is building a palace (*Mere Christianity,* 174).

This quote affected me deeply, and then there were the sleepless early morning hours when phrases of hymns would bless my mind. One of the most recurring songs was "I Will Follow God's Plan" (*Children's*

Songbook, 164). I would hear in my mind, "*I* will follow God's plan for me," "I *will* follow God's plan for me," "I will *follow* God's plan for me," I will follow *God's* plan for me," "I will follow God's *plan* for me," "I will follow God's plan for *me.*"

Sometimes in my mind I'd sing with determination:

> *My life is a gift; my life has a plan.*
> *My life has a purpose; in heav'n it began.*
> *My choice was to come to this lovely home on earth*
> *And seek for God's light to direct me from birth.*
> *I will follow God's plan for me,*
> *Holding fast to his word and his love.*
> *I will work, and I will pray;*
> *I will always walk in his way.*
> *Then I will be happy on earth*
> *And in my home above.*

Through these and so many more experiences, I've come to believe that "self-esteem" is a good attempt to help us, for a man-made philosophy. Most of the principles are true, but the emphasis, that self-esteem rests entirely on the individual, is wrong. The divine way, which could be termed "true self-esteem," I now believe, is to esteem my Maker and turn myself over to Him (allowing my sense of self to be strengthened as I am obedient to His will and accomplish my work as His child.) I will allow Him to do the repair work He deems necessary and set my sights on eternity rather than the worldly—the palace rather than the cottage. I do this by being willing to follow His plan for me.

Goethe said, "If God wanted me otherwise, He would have made me otherwise" (wisdom-and-philosophy.com). Applied: "If God wants me otherwise, He will make me otherwise, if only I will let Him."

FASTING:
A GLORIOUS PRINCIPLE

My child: "Mommy, is this the Sunday we have to hurry?"

Me: "Well, we don't want to be late for church."

My child: "No, Mommy, is this the Sunday we have to go fast?"

Teaching my children about the law of the fast was challenging. As a child I never questioned fasting. Some Sundays there was just no breakfast, and I accepted my parents' rules. I didn't have any real understanding of the law of the fast, however, until I taught it to my children, several of whom did have questions. From my study and application of the law in my life, I know that fasting is a true principle. It seems the more I live the law of the fast the better things go. I can't tell you anything specific, but somehow, someway, life is different in a good way.

I read the Church handbook on fasting. It says that fast day is observed properly by abstaining from food and drink for two consecutive meals, attending fast and testimony meeting, and giving a generous fast offering to help care for those in need. That's it! So the implementation questions, such as when should a child begin to participate in the fast, how soon should a child fast for two meals, what should be done when a woman is pregnant or nursing, can we still take pills, and when should a child begin paying fast offerings, is left to the individual and family to decide. This personal interpreting corresponds with the way Joseph Smith described how he governed the people: "I teach the people correct principles and they govern themselves" (*Journal of Discourses*, 10:57–58). I've found that the principle of fasting and personal answers to the above questions seem to be accepted easily when the components of purpose and prayer are emphasized. It's been said that fasting without purpose and prayer is simply dieting.

President David O. McKay said:

> Do not think that there is not a spiritual significance in the little principle of fasting. Do not think, parents, that you are favoring your child when, out of compassion, you say, "Oh, give him his breakfast; oh, let us have breakfast; let us have dinner; I have a headache; the little boy is too young to go without his meal," and so on. You do not know what you are doing by such teaching as that. I want to tell you that the children of our Church can be so taught this principle of self-denial that they will set worthy examples to their parents in the observance of it. (*Gospel Ideals*, 213)

Physical conditions may make it unwise to fast, but the spirit of the fast is too wonderful to miss unless absolutely necessary. I remember the Wilford Woodruff example: "It was remarked this morning that some people said they could not fast because it made their head ache. Well, I can fast, and so can any other man; and if it makes my head ache by keeping the commandments of God, let it ache" (*The Discourses of Wilford Woodruff*, 180). When I've been pregnant or nursing, I have participated in the spirit of the fast without technically fasting. I've done so by forgoing unnecessary foods such as potato chips, cookies, or other snacks and by eating only enough to keep from becoming ill.

The reasons to fast are many. I read that the Quorum of the Twelve Apostles set aside "a day of humiliation, fasting, praise, prayer and thanksgiving" (*HC,* 5:209) to express gratitude when Joseph Smith was released from prison in 1842. President Ezra Taft Benson said that you can gain a testimony through fasting and its companion, prayer: "Your first obligation is to get that testimony through prayer, through fasting" (*Teachings of Ezra Taft Benson*, 192–93). Alma reports that fasting is part of the grieving process: "And now surely this was a sorrowful day; yea, a time of solemnity, and a time of much fasting and prayer" (Alma 28:6). President Spencer W. Kimball taught that fasting helps you get closer to Heavenly Father: "To omit to do this righteous act of fasting would deprive us of these blessings . . . of inspiration . . . and closeness to our Heavenly Father" (*The Teachings of Spencer W. Kimball*, 144). And fasting not only benefits the person who fasts, but the poor as well. As President Heber J. Grant taught, "Every living soul among the Latter-day Saints that fasts two meals once a month will be benefited spiritually . . . in a wonderful way— and sufficient means will be in the hands of the bishops to take care of all the poor" (*Gospel Standards*, 123).

As the handbook indicated, paying a generous fast offering is essential to a proper observance of the fast. President Kimball said, "Sometimes we have been a bit penurious and figured that we had for breakfast one egg and that cost so many cents and then we give that to the Lord. I think that when we are affluent, as many of us are, that we ought to be very, very generous . . . and give, instead of the amount we saved by our two meals of fasting, perhaps much, much more—ten times more where we are in a position to do it" (*Conference Report*, Apr. 1974, 184).

President Gordon B. Hinckley stated: "Think . . . of what would happen if the principles of fast day and the fast offering were observed throughout the world. The hungry would be fed, the naked clothed, the homeless sheltered. Our burden of taxes would be lightened. The giver would not suffer but would be blessed by his small abstinence. A new measure of concern and unselfishness would grow in the hearts of people everywhere" ("The State of the Church," *Ensign*, May 1991, 52–53).

The prophet Isaiah states the blessings that accompany the fast:

> Is not this the fast that I have chosen? to loose the bands of wickedness, to undo the heavy burdens, and to let the oppressed go free, and that ye break every yoke? Is it not to deal thy bread to the hungry, and that thou bring the poor that are cast out to thy house? when thou seest the naked, that thou cover him; and that thou hide not thyself from thine own flesh? Then shall thy light break forth as the morning, and thine health shall spring forth speedily: and thy righteousness shall go before thee; the glory of the Lord

shall be thy rereward. Then shalt thou call, and the Lord shall answer; thou shalt cry, and he shall say, Here I am. If thou take away from the midst of thee the yoke, the putting forth of the finger, and speaking vanity; And if thou draw out thy soul to the hungry, and satisfy the afflicted soul; then shall thy light rise in obscurity, and thy darkness be as the noonday: And the Lord shall guide thee continually, and satisfy thy soul in drought, and make fat thy bones: and thou shalt be like a watered garden, and like a spring of water, whose waters fail not. (Isa. 58:6–11)

I want those blessings! I want to pray and have the Lord say, "Here I am."

PRIORITIES AND BALANCE

In a talk by Elder M. Russell Ballard, entitled "Keeping Life's Demands in Balance" (*Ensign*, May 1987, 13), he noted, "Sometimes we need a personal crisis to reinforce in our minds what we really value and cherish." But since none of us wants anything to do with "a personal crisis," is it possible to keep, as Elder Ballard added, "an honest, open self-examination, an awareness within as to who and what we want to be" without the crisis?

Elder Ballard also observed: "Coping with the complex and diverse challenges of everyday life . . . is not an easy task. . . . Many good people who care a great deal are trying very hard to maintain balance, but they sometimes feel overwhelmed and defeated." To remedy this, he suggested that an insightful way to keep priorities in focus is to review the covenants we have made with the Lord. This review will help us clearly see "where we need to repent and change our lives to ensure that we are worthy of the promises that accompany our covenants and sacred ordinances. Working out our own salvation requires good planning and a deliberate, valiant effort" (ibid., 13).

His ideas, adapted below, are very straightforward and so basic that the concepts can be overlooked.

- Set a regular time to think about your life and set your priorities. Write down daily tasks.

- Prayerfully set balanced and attainable goals, and work on them in order of importance.

- Make sure your financial life is in order, always remembering to pay a full tithing and avoid debt.

- Maintain balance by staying close to your spouse, children, relatives, and friends. Be gentle and loving in your communications with them.

- Strive to keep the Spirit of the Lord with you by studying the scriptures. Make studying the Book of Mormon a lifelong habit.

- Schedule time for the right amount of rest, exercise, and relaxation. Looking and feeling good increases your dignity and self-respect.

- Hold weekly family home evenings. Teach each other the gospel. Be careful not to drift out of this practice.

- Pray often as individuals. Pray often as families. Parents are to initiate regular family prayer.

What keeps me from doing the basics so that when a personal crisis comes, no reassessing of priorities is needed?

Is it conviction? Intellectually and spiritually I know that nothing is more important than personal righteousness and strong family ties. But in the busyness and complexity of living one twenty-four-hour day right after another, I am lulled into a false sense that there will always be another day, season, or cycle to correct or fine-tune whatever is unbalanced in my life. That's why crisis causes quick and serious adjusting of values. There isn't always a tomorrow.

Is it habit? I'd like to think that my selfish, unproductive, and self-defeating habits are inborn and involuntary, but they aren't. You and I have the ability and the power, with Heavenly Father's help, to change habits. It is not easy and may not be fun. Experts say it takes twenty-one repetitions to replace a bad habit with a better one. Making habits of Elder Ballard's list will be its own reward.

Is it lack of discipline? As noted earlier, discipline comes from the word *disciple*. As I am willing (and trying) to become a true disciple of Jesus Christ, discipline becomes inherently easier. When I serve Him and feel I am on His errand, the motivation to do and become grows stronger and stronger.

One way to determine your personal conviction, habit, and discipline levels is to answer some tough questions implied in Elder Ballard's list:

- Do I push "pause" on my busyness and take time to think, ponder, and meditate about my life and the direction of my future?

- Do I write down attainable goals? The Sunday of general conference might be a good time to evaluate the progress of the past six months and revise goals for the next six based on the emphasis of that general conference. Elder Ballard's suggestion that using the covenants you've made to pinpoint where more concentration is needed is a suggestion all should try.

- Do I pray morning and night and throughout the day to keep focused on the things of God, asking for His Spirit to accompany me and be in my home?

- Is my dependence on the word of God evident? Are the scriptures and the words of the living prophets my lifeline?

- Do my actions show my family that they are always my first priority? Do I never leave home without family prayer? Are Monday night and family home evening synonymous?

"Family" is likely the core reminder that comes with crisis. The quote above the entrance to Primary Children's Medical Center in Salt Lake City reads, "The child first and always." Extend the concept to family: "The family first and always." As you think "family first" you'll move closer toward the balance Elder Ballard advised. In this singular effort you have to be more prayerful, more dependent on the Spirit, more financially disciplined, more dependent on the scriptures, more drawn to the words of the living prophets, more physically fit, and more focused on how your example will make an impact on the future—tomorrow, next month, and into eternity.

HUSBAND:
HOW IMPORTANT IS HE?

Dr. Laura Schlessinger wrote the book *The Proper Care and Feeding of Husbands.* Her message is simple: Wives, make your husband and marriage your top priority. She uses three "A" words to describe how a woman should treat her man—with approval, appreciation, and affection. She says that many wives are selfish, expecting or demanding that their husband fill their every need, want, and dream to the extreme, but not being willing to fill the basic needs of their husbands. She says that many wives view their husband as an annoyance and distraction who keeps them from more pressing and important matters.

Dr. Schlessinger suggests that such wives will remain unfulfilled because the way a wife is fulfilled is by putting her marriage first. She teaches that by filling a husband's needs, the wife's needs, perhaps even her wants and desires, will also be fulfilled. She makes the assertion that some wives treat total strangers with more respect than they do their husband.

Is this concept revolutionary? Yes, for women who bought into the false philosophies of the "liberated woman," as Dr. Schlessinger freely admits she once did, and perhaps even for women in the Church who have been tainted by these beliefs. In the Worldwide Leadership Training Meeting on January 10, 2004, President James E. Faust gave the following statistics:

Between 1970 and 2001, the marriage rate in the United States declined from 76.5 percent to 45.6 percent. The major factors contributing to this decline are young people delaying marriage, increases in the proportion of adult population who have never married, and an increase in cohabitation.

Since 1960, in the United States there has been a 760 percent increase in unmarried couples living together, amounting to 3.8 million couples in the year 2000. Most cohabitations end without marriage and are relatively short. Statistics show that cohabiting couples are much more likely to break up than are married couples.

Experts project that about half of the women in the United States will have a marriage dissolve some time in their life.

Out-of-wedlock births have increased by 158 percent.

Also disturbing is the shift in attitude about the purpose of marriage. More and more young people view marriage as a couples relationship, designed to fulfill the emotional needs of adults, rather than an institution for bringing up children. The pursuit of such "soul mate" relationships may well weaken marriage as an institution for rearing children.

Another disturbing challenge to the family is that children are becoming less valued. In many parts of the world, people are having fewer children. Abortion is probably the clearest sign that couples do not want children. An estimated quarter of all pregnancies worldwide end by induced abortion. The rates range from a high of almost 50 percent in Europe to about 15 percent in Africa (see Worldwide Leadership Training Meeting Report, 1–2).

Millions of mothers have become full-time employees, leaving husbands to fend for themselves, leaving babies and younger children in day care, and leaving older children to a latchkey existence. "Leaving" is the operative word, as a woman in the workplace often creates her world around her career, focusing mental and emotional energy outside the home. "Leaving" may also occur physically as a woman in the workforce is many, many times more likely to have an affair than is a stay-at-home mother (see Brenda Hunter, *Home by Choice*).

Abortion and fatherlessness also combine to disrupt marriages. Women (I can't call them mothers) have killed more than a million babies by abortion each year since 1973. The total is 35 million, which is many times greater than all Americans who have died in all wars combined, according to bible.com/abortstats. Another website, first-things.org, states, "Current trends indicate that by the year 2015 one of every two American babies will be born to a single mother, and illegitimacy will surpass divorce as the main cause of fatherlessness." And "more than 70 percent of juveniles in state reform institutions come from fatherless homes" (Jennifer E. Marshall, *Sanctioning Illegitimacy: Our National Character Is at Stake,* Family Research Council, 3/28/97).

In an environmentally conscious world where spotted owls have their habitats protected, it seems strange that the pillar of society—marriage and family—is being allowed to move toward extinction. The sum total of negative consequences to individuals and to society of this tragedy, whose founders are penthouse residents of the great and spacious building, cannot be overstated. Men are the losers. Women are the losers. And the children who suffer neglect, without sufficient nurture, grow up to repeat the cycle because nothing else is modeled for them. When "The Family: A Proclamation to the World" was issued in 1995, I thought it was good and important. Today I view it as nothing short of prophetically timely.

Prophets and Apostles have taught and warned, pleaded and begged for wives and mothers to heed the Lord's counsel regarding their divine role and the sacred nature of families. The Lord's way is described in the proclamation on the family. "By divine design, fathers are to preside over their families in love and righteousness and are responsible to provide the necessities of life and protection for their families. Mothers are primarily responsible for the nurture of their children."

When the world's way takes precedence over the Lord's way, even in the Church, two fatal malignancies that go basically unnoticed take root in families, just as the frog doesn't notice the water getting hotter and hotter until he is boiled and dead. First, respect for the priesthood of God declines. And second, when women allow reverence for priesthood bearers to be watered down, there is a subsequent decline in the number and volume of promptings from the Holy Ghost in their lives.

The value men should have in women's eyes is beautifully illustrated in the following story:

> Variations of the tale are found in the folklore of Eastern Europe, but it was said to have happened during the Middle Ages in Germany. The year was 1141 and Wolf, the duke of Bavaria, was besieged inside his castle of Weinsberg by the army of Frederick and his brother, the

emperor Konrad. The siege had lasted long and Wolf realized he had no choice but to surrender. Messengers rode back and forth, terms were proposed, conditions allowed, and arrangements completed. Wolf and his army prepared to give themselves over to their bitter enemy.

But the wives of Weinsberg were not prepared to lose everything. They sent a message to Konrad, asking the governor to promise safe passage for all women in the garrison, that they might come out with as many of their valuables as they could carry on their backs.

The request was graciously granted, and soon the castle gates opened. Out came the women—but not as supposed. They carried neither gold nor jewels on their backs, but each one of them was bending under the weight of her husband, whom she hoped to save from the vengeance of the conquering army. Konrad was so moved by this extraordinary act that he made peace with the duke of Bavaria on much more favorable terms than expected. The castle mount was afterward known as the Hill of Weibertreue, or "woman's fidelity." (Mark H. Creech, "The Wives of Weinsberg," AgapePress, lifeway.com)

Is such a feat possible today? Yes—if I, and you, begin today to give more appreciation, affection, and approval to the men whose last names we took upon ourselves. I need to respect him and treasure him and support him as he presides over our family. "The family is ordained of God. Marriage between man and woman is essential to His eternal plan. Children are entitled to birth within the bonds of matrimony, and to be reared by a father and a mother who honor marital vows with complete fidelity. Happiness in family life is most likely to be achieved when founded upon the teachings of the Lord Jesus Christ" ("The Family: A Proclamation to the World").

How valuable is my husband to me, to my children, to my children's children? I can answer that question with another question: Is there anything more important?

GRANDMOTHERING

I'm in the age group where most of my friends are grandmas. Grandmother number one tends her daughter's children weekdays while her daughter, whose husband was injured in an accident, works. Grandmother number two lives across country from her grandchildren and does her grandmothering by e-mail, phone, and visits every other year. Grandmother number three drives forty-five minutes each Sunday to another town to take her grandchildren to church in their ward, an activity her son and daughter-in-law approve of but have no inclination to do themselves. Grandmother number four lives next door to her grandchildren and is like a second mother, taking them to lessons, driving paper routes with them, experiencing life with them daily. Grandmother number five is separated from her grandchildren by a thousand miles and a bitter divorce. Her influence is limited to whatever she can do by mail. And to complicate life, many grandmothers do all of the above, because they are grandmother to children in several different families. But what I observe about each grandma is that whatever the situation, what she does best is respond to and fulfill needs.

My experience of grandmothering is compounded by the fact that I am still a mother or mother-in-law to my grandchildren's parents. Grandmothers will feel the need to be at the sides of their grandchildren but also still need to be at the sides of their children to offer physical, spiritual, and emotional support. Adult children often appreciate some mothering even when they are parents themselves. I visit my mother, who is in her mid-eighties, just to feel her love. I've had to stop myself from allowing her to do things for me that I should be doing for her. I feel so blessed to have known a mother's love.

Grandmothers help by taking a turn sitting with a hospitalized child, watching younger children while mother gets a much-needed nap or has a chance to run errands alone, taking children to the zoo, spending an afternoon cleaning a closet with them, paying for the turkey for a special meal, or reading with a struggling youngster. She can fill in when, where, and however she is needed as an extra set of hands or a sympathetic listening ear. She prays for promptings to know when she is needed and how to fill that need and show concern while not offending or taking away stewardship from her adult child or her son- or daughter-in-law.

Mothers who have parented by the Spirit know the blessing of grandmothering by the Spirit. A grandmother told of the evening she was unloading the dishwasher two thousand miles from her eleven-year-old granddaughter, Marcie. Marcie's family had recently moved from a small, family-oriented town to one of the largest cities in the world. Marcie had become fearful of going to school and seemed emotionally paralyzed. Her parents were nearly to the point of taking her for counseling. At this moment, Marcie's mother had just told Marcie that Heavenly Father loved her and that the Holy Ghost would comfort her and bless her no matter where she lived. Marcie's mother suggested that she kneel and ask Heavenly Father to help her overcome her fears. As Marcie dropped to her knees and the tears began to fall, Marcie's mother knelt beside her, silently pleading that somehow Marcie would know her prayers were heard. Also at that very minute, her brothers and father were downstairs installing a new modem, tying up the telephone line.

Suddenly the grandmother had a thought: *Call Marcie.* She went to the phone and dialed the number. It was busy. She went back to unloading the dishwasher. Again the thought came. She went to the phone. This time she got through, but could hear her son-in-law and grandsons talking about the new modem. She couldn't make them hear her. She went back to unloading the dishwasher. The idea came again to call Marcie. She dialed the number for the third time and her son-in-law answered and began to have a nice-to-hear-from-you chat. The grandmother said, "I've called to talk to Marcie." When Marcie came to the phone, Grandmother could hear in her voice that things weren't going well. It was then Grandmother realized that she had been prompted to call. She quickly prayed for wisdom to say the right things in the right way. It wasn't until several hours later, however, when her daughter called to tell the details, that the miracle was pieced together. The grandmother humbly acknowledged the prompting and the opportunity to be of service at a crucial moment—even two thousand miles away.

Such a grandma is described in 2 Timothy 1:5. The Apostle Paul refers in this verse to Timothy's grandmother: "When I call to remembrance the unfeigned faith that is in thee, which dwelt first in thy grandmother Lois . . ." A grandmother's example of faith and testimony, spoken and silent, is the most important work she will ever do.

Virginia H. Pearce, President Gordon B. Hinckley's daughter, said, "My grandmother was worried about my religious training at an early age, as most are. So she took it upon herself to read me the Bible every time I went to visit her. As she read, she always added her own interpretations. She often said, 'Pretty is as pretty does. Beauty is only skin deep (she firmly believed that); it is what's inside that really makes you beautiful'" (*Glimpses into the Life and Heart of Marjorie Pay*, 243). Grandmothers are teachers whose counsel sticks in the minds of their grandchildren.

My grandchildren delight and challenge me. I know you will, or do now, love your grandchildren. I've also learned that you and I both have the cutest grandchildren. All children are precious gifts. I like to read to them and watch them draw with chalk on the sidewalk. I like to go on little excursions with them and to bake with them. And, I've been known to enjoy working with them. Somehow, they think working at grandma's is more fun than working at home. Grandmothering provides two great blessings—to feel the love of a child and to have an opportunity to influence another generation.

All this said, there are times I am tired and appreciate their parents taking them home. I so appreciate the consideration I get from my children (both by birth and by marriage). Sometimes some of my friends feel somewhat put upon by some of their married children. *Some* was used three times in that sentence to emphasize that *some* of the time grandmothers need their own lives. They are willing to help, but their children shouldn't overuse them. They are older and deserve respect. Don't think you are doing Grandma a favor by having her babysit for you. She is doing you the favor. She already raised a family. Call in advance. Be sensitive and careful of her time, energy, and feelings. There is very good motivation for you to treat your mother or mother-in-law with the greatest respect, because the consideration you show to them will be shown to you in a few years. Your children are watching how you treat your mother and mother-in-law, and in the future will treat you as you treat them.

I thought about my grandmas—Nellie Todd and Emma Haymore. Grandma Todd taught me sacrifice. Grandpa and Grandma Todd bought a beautiful new home for about $5,000 in 1922. Then, during World War II, my father got married and served Uncle Sam in New York City and in the Philippine Islands. During that time my sister and I were born. When the war was over, Grandpa and Grandma Todd invited our family to come live with them. This was their arrangement: we lived upstairs in the lovely home and Grandpa and Grandma moved downstairs to a small apartment in the basement! As I grew up, my sisters and I were frequent visitors to her little apartment. She graciously entertained us and always offered us toast buttered on both sides!

From my Grandmother Haymore I learned to make do and do without, and to love to write. The year I was going into fifth grade she made eight new school dresses for me. She had me try on each one. As I was admiring her work and thanking her, she told me where she got the fabric, ribbon, lace, buttons, zippers, snaps, etc. Nothing was purchased at a store. She had made the dresses from bits and pieces of clothing that no longer fit someone else! She also loved to write—poems for all occasions and her thoughts on multitudes of topics. When she was in her seventies, she compiled her writings into a set of volumes called *Brass Tacks and Knickknacks.*

I wonder what my grandchildren will remember about me.

THE HOLY GHOST: MOTHERING BY THE SPIRIT

Being a mother is such an overwhelming responsibility that I feel inadequate on a daily basis. The sacred obligation and opportunity to mold a child of God into a responsible adult, who will in time parent other children of God, is awesome and burdensome. What to say, when to say it, how to say it, what to leave unsaid, what is really being taught, and what the long-range consequences will be are just a few of the issues that often befuddle my brain. Heavenly Father in His omniscience knew that you and I and every other woman who cares for children would need guidance, incremental wisdom, deep understanding, and discerning sensitivity. How does He provide this help? He directs worthy mothers and others who help children through the influence of the Holy Ghost. It is He, the third member of the Godhead, who helps receptive mothers in countless ways—comforting, teaching, and bringing ideas to their minds.

Seeking the help of the Holy Ghost. A mother told me of an experience she had of catching her child telling a series of lies. She sat the child on a stool in front of her and said, "Stay right there and don't move." Then she went into another room, knelt down, and asked her Father in Heaven how she should discipline the child. She asked for an appropriate punishment and for the right words so that her child would correct the behavior and become a person of integrity. She told me of the blessings that came in that instance and others as she has taken the time to ask for the Holy Ghost's influence in her parenting.

How valuable is a prompting or impression from the Holy Ghost? Those fortunate Nephites who were blessed to be at the temple in

Bountiful on the day the risen Lord blessed their children desired one thing more: "And they did pray for that which they most desired; and they desired that the Holy Ghost should be given unto them" (3 Ne. 19:9). Do you desire the Holy Ghost? As baptized and confirmed members of the Church, you and I have received the Holy Ghost. If I want Him to actively help me in my parenting, I must ask for His influence. I must ask, as illustrated in the story, for the wisdom to deal with this child in that situation. Beginning with the partaking of the sacrament each week, I try to remember to ask for His Spirit to be with me.

George Q. Cannon said:

> It is the privilege of the Latter-day Saints to have revelation. . . . And this is the way to receive it. This is the way that the Church of Christ is guided. Many suppose that the Lord, when He wants a thing done, sends His angels to tell us what to do. He may do so under certain circumstances, but the guide that God has given unto the Presidency of this Church and unto the Apostles and unto all who stand in responsible stations is the Spirit of God, the Holy Ghost. It is by its guidance and by the light which it gives that this Church is led. And it is obtained by waiting patiently for the Lord to make known His will and preparing ourselves for it, asking Him to give it. It comes then in power. It comes with the clearness of the light of the sun. It comes overpoweringly so that there can be no doubt left in the mind as to the correctness of the course. (*Gospel Truth*, 1:333–34)

Hearing the voice of the Spirit. But is the still, small voice ever too still and too small? The prophet Elijah teaches where *not* to look for the voice of the Holy Ghost. "And, behold, the Lord passed by, and a great and strong wind rent the mountains, and brake in pieces the rocks before the Lord; but the Lord was not in the wind: and after the wind an earthquake; but the Lord was not in the earthquake: And after the earthquake a fire; but the Lord was not in the fire: and after the fire a still small voice" (1 Kgs. 19:11–12). The still, small voice is symbolically found not in wind, earthquake, or fire. The voice of the Spirit is still and small—quiet, soft, gentle. He doesn't yell or coerce or threaten. He whispers. Promptings don't usually come as clearly as writings on the wall, and, personally, there is much to keep me from hearing the voice of the Holy Ghost. When I'm too busy, too stressed, or too determined to do things my own way, I often miss His call, and He doesn't leave messages on voice mail. The more I fail to hear, the softer His voice will become and the fewer and farther between will be His promptings.

What drives the Spirit away? President Ezra Taft Benson illustrated a great hindrance to hearing the still, small voice. "For the Holy Ghost to be fully operative we have to keep our channels clear of sin. The clearer our channels, the easier it is to receive God's message to us; and the more of His messages we receive and put into action, the greater will be our joy. If our channels are not clear of sin, then we may think we have received inspiration on a matter when it is really promptings from the devil" (*The Teachings of Ezra Taft Benson*, 76). Such behaviors as irreverent thoughts and actions; breaking any commandments; allowing oneself to feel arrogance, anger, envy, pride, malice, intolerance; or a desire to retaliate all repel the Spirit.

What creates an atmosphere conducive to inspiration? When I allow my mind to be both still (peaceful or quiet) and small—that is, humble and teachable, willing to take counsel, realizing my infinitesimal smallness and relative nothingness—then I notice that I can tune in and receive His signal. In a Gospel Doctrine class, a man commented that it had been his experience that women seemed to be more attuned to promptings from the Holy Ghost than men. Though this is arguable, the class responded with interesting stories to support the idea. For instance, a brother told of an instance when he and his wife were observing a situation. He explained that it was his wife who heard the voice of the Spirit and was alerted to a potential tragedy that was seconds away. Her response to the still, small voice caused her to take immediate and decisive action that saved a child from certain death. The class pondered why women might, at times, be more attuned to the whispering of the Spirit. Then, a woman who I feel has acute spiritual sensitivity raised her hand and explained that her clearest messages from the Holy Ghost had come while she was ironing or doing the dishes. Other women concurred. The consensus of the class was that quiet moments allow promptings to be felt and heard, and that perhaps women have potentially more *quiet* built into their lives as many women are home doing mundane chores or driving carpools or waiting for a child to return from some activity.

From the limited experience I've had with the Holy Ghost, I know how marvelous His promptings are. My goal is to have His constant companionship as promised in Doctrine and Covenants 121:46, "The Holy Ghost shall be thy constant companion." I also know how to receive more attention from the Holy Ghost. He is like any other guest. If He doesn't feel comfortable in my home (my heart and soul), He will not visit me. And I must invite Him in. I am working on building more quiet into my life. Lorenzo Snow said:

> In order to arrive at the state of perfection . . . we must be true men and true women; we must have faith largely developed, and we must be worthy of the companionship of the Holy Ghost to aid us in the work of righteousness all the day long, to enable us to sacrifice our own will to the will of the Father, to battle against our fallen nature, and to do right for the love of doing right, keeping our eye single to the honor and glory of God. To do this there must be an inward feeling of the mind that is conscious of the responsibility that we are under, that recognizes the fact that the eye of God is upon us and that our every act and the motives that prompt it must be accounted for; and we must be constantly en rapport with the Spirit of the Lord. (*Journal of Discourses*, 23:190–91)

It's a fact: the voice of the Holy Ghost is *still* and *small*. As with the Nephites, it is a voice I desire. Speaking to my children as the Spirit speaks to me—I got the idea a few years ago that I could emulate the ways in which the Holy Ghost speaks to me and use those ways to speak to my children. I try to remember to ask myself, do the words *still* and *small* accurately describe how I am speaking? When I do this, communication between my children and me improves. (It also works well with husbands, just in case you're wondering.)

The idea actually came because of an experience I had one day when I lost my voice. I could not even whisper. Even without being able to talk, I still had to walk the mile to the elementary school to get six-year-old Matt and five-year-old Michelle, and I had to bring with me three-year-old Mike and eighteen-month-old Anne, who was in a stroller. The reason I had to walk to retrieve the two older children from school was because we were new to the neighborhood, city, and country. We had been transferred to England, and I hadn't yet made connections to carpool. We had only one car, and Richard needed it this particular day. So off I went with no voice to guide these children across major streets, a park, and through several neighborhoods. I had prayed and was praying with every step because I couldn't yell if there was danger or caution the children about running ahead, hiding, risk taking, and lingering behind, which were all things that had happened on other days.

As soon as the children realized I had no voice, astonishingly, they did not *need* my voice. They stayed right beside me. They seemed to enjoy the peace and beauties of the fall day, shared their experiences in school, and asked what they could do to help fix dinner when we got home. The spell lasted several days until my voice returned. In analyzing the situation, I realized that a quieter, gentler voice was more likely to draw my children closer me than my usual drill-sergeant approach. I thought of the Holy Ghost and His comforting, suggesting, hinting, leading, teaching, warning, enlightening, testifying ways—all done with a still, small voice.

I treasure a prompting from the Holy Ghost. In turbulent times as I've fasted and begged for help, He has, on occasion, reminded me of a scripture phrase or the words of a hymn or has guided my thinking. He has helped me understand doctrine and blessed me with testimony. What He has done for me, I should try to do for my children. Where would I be if the Holy Ghost left me on my own? With slight extension of the words in Doctrine and Covenants 121, I feel that I should speak to my children with persuasion, with long-suffering, with gentleness and meekness, and with love unfeigned; with kindness, and pure knowledge. This scripture says there will be occasions when a parent must correct a child, but afterward the parent should show "an increase of love toward him whom thou hast reproved" (see vv. 41–43). I feel I am duty bound to teach, enlighten, comfort, testify and to share wisdom, knowledge, and experience with my children, all through the influence of the Holy Ghost. The Holy Ghost can also tell me when to stop talking. The word in the scriptures is *constrained.* There may be those times the prompting comes, "Don't say any more. Tell him you love him and go to bed."

It follows that as I try to follow the example of the Holy Ghost and speak to others as He speaks to me, angry words are never part of the equation. The scriptures warn of anger: "Cease from anger, and forsake wrath" (Ps. 37:8); "he that is soon angry dealeth foolishly" (Prov. 14:17); "provoke not your children to anger" (Col. 3:21); and most to the point, Proverbs 15:1, "A soft answer turneth away wrath." If you meet anger in a child, respond softly—in volume, in demeanor, in message. It is impossible to hear promptings that may come from the Holy Ghost to guide you through a moment of crisis if you submit to anger.

The omniscience of the Holy Ghost gives Him an enviable view. In this earthly state, you and I have to compensate by constant vigilance. One of the ways I think I can increase my understanding of what my children need and how and when to teach, lead, guide, warn, enlighten, and testify (hopefully never all at the same time) is to listen to them. This doesn't come naturally to me. I talk *way too much*. I want and try to remember that one way to encourage my children to talk to me is by being quiet. Silence may feel awkward, but it may encourage the child or teen to talk to you. I've tried to create such situations by taking them, one at a time, on errands to give them an opportunity to talk and for me to listen. I've incorporated a ready supply of encouraging comments such as "Oh?" "Really!" "Is that right?" "How interesting." "How do you feel about that?" "Is there a way I can help?" My goal is to do less than half of the talking. The higher the ratio in the child's favor, the better the communication. When I am at home and a child says something to me, I know I should stop whatever I'm doing and give him or her eye contact. I know my face is my child's mirror. I need my face and eyes to reflect, "I'm listening. What you say is important to me."

Sounds simple on paper, but I've found that listening takes effort and the discipline not to jump in, give quick advice, and move on.

Listening takes concentration and control, but as I listen to my children and invite the Spirit to be part of our conversations, a three-way conversation is the result. Could there be a better method? How grateful I am for the Holy Ghost, His influence in my life, and His example of ways to better communicate with my children.

THERE IS ALWAYS HOPE

Motherhood is often a lonely experience. When you feel alone, as if you are at the bottom of everyone's pecking order, think of the word *hope*. Hope is, of the three great gospel principles, always found in the middle—faith, *hope*, charity. Hope, sandwiched between faith and charity, is often more like a conjunction than an essential noun. Below is an analysis of the three principles to see what role hope really plays.

Faith. Faith is an interesting and important word. My understanding of "faith" as a concept increased when it was pointed out to me that *faith* is not the first principle of the gospel, according to the forth article of faith. The first principle of the gospel is faith *in the Lord Jesus Christ. Faith* never stands alone. Faith in the Lord Jesus Christ is how motherhood is less lonely. Faith in Jesus Christ, in His words, in His Atonement, in His Church, in His prophets is the foundation of hope. Helaman said to his sons: "And now, my sons, remember, remember that it is upon the rock of our Redeemer, who is Christ, the Son of God, that ye must build your foundation; that when the devil shall send forth his mighty winds, yea, his shafts in the whirlwind, yea, when all his hail and his mighty storm shall beat upon you, it shall have no power over you to drag you down to the gulf of misery and endless wo, because of the rock upon which ye are built, which is a sure foundation, a foundation whereon if men build they cannot fall" (Hel. 5:12).

Charity. Mother gives and gives and gives—as wife to her husband, as mother to her children, as daughter to her parents, and as sister to her siblings, to her sisters in the gospel, and to the poor and needy. She shares, goes without, and stretches all available resources, especially herself. She tries to love as Christ loves. She knows how important charity is and works hard at obtaining it. (Charity is a gift of the Spirit that allows a person to become truly Christlike.)

Hope. *Hope* is the word in between faith and charity. Hope can be the balm to every wound. When there seems to be nothing else, there is always hope. Hope is why we have faith and charity.

One too-busy mother, facing severe adversity, told of her prayers, fasting, and temple sessions to petition her Father in Heaven for help. "I often feel so overwhelmed and so burdened in my many roles," she said. "But once in a while, when I'm feeling helpless and hopeless, I have been blessed by reassuring thoughts from hymns that come unsolicited into my brain. One morning my first waking thought was 'Oh know ye not that angels attend you.' I felt a surge of hope and throughout the day tried to remember why those words were familiar to me. Later I began singing the melody to the hymn 'Come unto Jesus.' I turned to number 117 in the hymnbook and read the words. 'Come unto Jesus, ye heavy laden.' It's in the third verse that the words are found with one change. In the hymn the words are 'Oh, know you not that angels are near you.' Instead of *are near* I heard *attend.* Not only are angels near me, they attend me!"

She continued, "On another occasion, in an equally challenging situation, as I sang with the congregation 'We Thank Thee, O God, for a Prophet,' the second verse seemed like personal revelation: 'When dark clouds of trouble hang o'er us, And threaten our peace to destroy, There is hope smiling brightly before us, And we know that deliverance is nigh.' There is hope smiling brightly before me! My deliverance is nigh! Another infusion of hope.

"Many months later, I was blessed by another hope-filled 'hymn thought.' This time the words were 'Lead, kindly light, amid the encircling gloom. Lead thou me on.' This message was a precursor of things yet to happen. As the 'encircling gloom' gathered seemingly exponentially, I still could feel hopeful. I knew I was being watched out for and would be protected and provided for. What a good definition of hope—the feeling, expectation, and optimism that I am known by God and that He will lead me on through the darkness of the unknown. Hope is the match lit in a dark room, the light that leads us through murky times."

But there is a deeper, doctrinal hope that makes hope even more important and something to cling to. From the *Encyclopedia of Mormonism:*

> The concept of hope plays a vital role in Latter-day Saint thought. Firmly centered in Christ and his resurrection . . . the "hope of eternal life" (Titus 1:2) . . . is the opposite of the despair found among those who are "without Christ, having no hope, and without God in the world" (Eph. 2:12). As . . . Moroni writes, "If ye have no hope, ye must needs be in despair" (Moro. 10:22). For those, however, who accept Christ's Atonement and resurrection, there comes a "brightness of hope" (2 Ne. 31:20) through which all who believe in God "might with surety hope for a better world" (Ether 12:4).
>
> The scriptures employ the term "hope" in a variety of ways. Some usages suggest desire, such as the statement in Article of Faith 13 that "we believe all things, we *hope* all things, we have endured many things, and *hope* to be able to endure all things (italics added)." Others denote firm expectation, such as Paul's description of Abraham "who against hope believed in hope, that he might become the father of many nations" (Rom. 4:18). . . .
>
> Regardless of their form, the individual variations of meaning all center on the confidence or trust in God that springs from knowledge that mankind is saved through the Atonement ("for we are saved by hope," [Rom. 8:24]). Hence, hope is inseparably connected with faith. Book of Mormon passages add insight to the New Testament. . . . "How is it that ye can attain unto faith, save ye shall have hope?" (Moro. 7:40); "hope cometh of faith" (Ether 12:4); "without faith there cannot be any hope" (Moro. 7:42). It

is also an essential attitude for individual salvation . . .
"Man must hope, or he cannot receive an inheritance in
the place which thou hast prepared" (Ether 12:32)."
(3:656)

Hope is essential on every level. Think of hope to dispel gloom
"when dark clouds of trouble hang o'er you." Hope that "your deliverance is nigh." Hope, knowing that angels are nearby and attending
you. Hope in the Light of Christ. When there seems to be nothing
else, there is always hope.

MODESTY:
DO YOU WORSHIP AT
THE SHRINE OF FASHION?

The organization for young women in the Church began at the home of Brigham Young with the establishment of the Cooperative Retrenchment Association in November 1869. Besides the call to the young women to be industrious, to refrain from gossip, and to grow spiritually, President Young asked them "to retrench from the styles of the world in dress and deportment, and thus to be proper examples of Latter-day Saints."

By 1870 each ward in Salt Lake Valley had its own similar young women's organization with its own stated resolutions. The "one central thought" in all resolutions was "electing a greater simplicity of dress and of living; and . . . cultivating the mind rather than ministering to the pleasure of the body." For example, the Fourteenth Ward resolved: "Feeling that we have worshipped at the shrine of fashion too long [we] do solemnly pledge ourselves to retrench in our dress, and to wear only that which is becoming to women professing to be Saints" (*Encyclopedia of Mormonism*, 4:1616).

Modesty remains a crucial issue today. Choosing the world's ways or the Lord's way is a choice every girl and woman makes each time she sews, purchases an article of clothing, or every time she gets dressed. It's plain to see who is on the Lord's side. Young Women leaders and mothers have the responsibility to set the example. What is the standard?

Prophets have warned every generation against moral decay. In 1972 President Spencer W. Kimball counseled:

> One contributing factor to immodesty and a breakdown of
> moral values is the modern dress. I am sure that the

immodest clothes that are worn by some of our young women, and their mothers, contribute directly and indirectly to the immorality of this age. Even fathers sometimes encourage it. I wonder if our young sisters realize the temptation they are flaunting before young men when they leave their bodies partly uncovered. They frequently wear short skirts and body-revealing blouses and sweaters that seem to be worn to draw attention to the form of the girl and to emphasize sexuality. (*Faith Precedes the Miracle*, 163)

President Gordon B. Hinckley said to the young women of the Church:

Modesty in dress and manner will assist in protecting against temptation. It may be difficult to find modest clothing, but it can be found with enough effort. I sometimes wish every girl had access to a sewing machine and training in how to use it. She could then make her own attractive clothing. I suppose this is an unrealistic wish. But I do not hesitate to say that you can be attractive without being immodest. You can be refreshing and buoyant and beautiful in your dress and in your behavior. Your appeal to others will come of your personality, which is the sum of your individual characteristics. Be happy. Wear a smile. Have fun. But draw some rigid parameters, a line in the sand, as it were, beyond which you will not go. ("Stay on the High Road," *Ensign*, May 2004, 112)

What are those "rigid parameters"? The Church's pamphlet *For the Strength of Youth* states: "Immodest clothing includes short shorts and skirts, tight clothing, shirts that do not cover the stomach, and other revealing attire. Young women should wear clothing that covers the shoulder and avoid clothing that is low-cut in the front or the back or revealing in any other manner. Young men should also maintain modesty in their appearance. All should avoid extremes in clothing, appearance, and hairstyle" (*For the Strength of Youth*, 14–16).

From a *Liahona* article:

> Today more than ever before, our children need clear guid-
> ance in dressing modestly. In many modern societies, stan-
> dards of modesty and even decency in dress have all but
> vanished. Styles that once might have been seen only in a
> cocktail lounge or an inappropriate magazine are now
> being marketed to children—and at younger and younger
> ages. So waiting until our children approach their teens to
> teach them about modesty is waiting too long. (Jan
> Pinborough, "Everything Good and Beautiful," *Liahona,*
> Mar. 2003, 14)

The Church would have more influence on the world if the girls
and women of the Church would pledge as did the Fourteenth Ward
so many years ago, "Feeling that we have worshipped at the shrine of
fashion too long [we] do solemnly pledge ourselves to retrench in our
dress, and to wear only that which is becoming to women professing
to be Saints."

A million rules could be set about how many inches of clothing
need to cover what areas of the body, but the Lord makes it simple. He
has given the standard; it is the temple garment. Whether you have
been to the temple or not, you will be modest if you wear clothes that
cover the areas the garment covers. Girls will accept this standard as the
pattern set by the Lord when they are taught this principle from their
earliest youth. Each girl will know she is a child of God. She will understand that boys grow up to be fathers and girls grow up to be mothers.
It will seem logical that Heavenly Father designed bodies for a sacred
purpose and that after a man and a woman marry, they become partners with Him to bring more of His children to earth. Each young girl
can understand that by dressing modestly she shows both respect to
Heavenly Father and gratitude to Him for her body. She can be taught,
as President Kimball said, that members of the Church of Jesus Christ
don't need to follow the world's idea of what is fashionable, that it's
good to be different and create her own modest style.

The Apostle Paul in his first letter to the people in Corinth wrote:
"What? know ye not that your body is the temple of the Holy Ghost

which is in you, which ye have of God, and ye are not your own? For ye are bought with a price: therefore glorify God in your body, and in your spirit, which are God's" (1 Cor. 6:19–20).

As our girls grow into young women, they can be taught, as the scripture says, that their bodies are temples and that life is a test to see how well they will care for their bodies.

The temple garment is the standard for our children to prepare for and for us to honor. Proper wearing of the garment provides a shield of protection. A good reminder about garments is this letter to priesthood leaders from the First Presidency, dated October 10, 1988:

> Church members who have been clothed with the garment in the temple have made a covenant to wear it throughout their lives. This has been interpreted to mean that it is worn as underclothing both day and night. This sacred covenant is between the member and the Lord. Members should seek the guidance of the Holy Spirit to answer for themselves any personal questions about the wearing of the garment. . . . The promise of protection and blessings is conditioned upon worthiness and faithfulness in keeping the covenant.

> The fundamental principle ought to be to wear the garment and not to find occasions to remove it. Thus, members should not remove either all or part of the garment to work in the yard or to lounge around the home in swimwear or immodest clothing. Nor should they remove it to participate in recreational activities that can reasonably be done with the garment worn properly beneath regular clothing. When the garment must be removed, such as for swimming, it should be restored as soon as possible.

> The principles of modesty and keeping the body appropriately covered are implicit in the covenant and should govern the nature of all clothing worn. Endowed members of the Church wear the garment as a reminder of the sacred

covenants they have made with the Lord and also as a protection against temptation and evil. How it is worn is an outward expression of an inward commitment to follow the Savior.

(For an excellent article on the subject, read Elder Carlos E. Asay, "The Temple Garment: 'An Outward Expression of an Inward Commitment,'" *Ensign,* Aug. 1977, 19.)

BELIEVE CHRIST—YOUR MOST IMPORTANT WORK

Circumstances vary and life experiences are diverse, but the most important work you will ever do is to show that no matter what life throws at you, the gospel of Jesus Christ works. If you have a husband who isn't a good father, provider, support, Church member, faithful spouse; or if you have a handicapped child (or children) or a rebellious child (or children) who consume a disproportionate share of time, resources, and energy; or if you struggle with your own health, finances, or with relationships in your own family or family by marriage, you can, despite all the adversity and trauma, be a living testimony that the principles of the gospel of Jesus Christ work in your life. You can say as Helaman did, "That it is upon the rock of [my] Redeemer, who is Christ, the Son of God, that [I] must build [my] foundation; that when the devil shall send forth his mighty winds, yea, his shafts in the whirlwind, yea, when all his hail and his mighty storm shall beat upon [me], it shall have no power over [me] to drag [me] down to the gulf of misery and endless wo, because of the rock upon which [I am] built, which is a sure foundation, a foundation whereon if [I] build [I] cannot fall" (Hel. 5:12).

When you show by example and precept that the Ten Commandments work today, that the Beatitudes really make life *blessed,* that the gospel of Jesus Christ was restored to the Prophet Joseph Smith, and that each succeeding prophet has been God's mouthpiece on earth, you help your child build on the Rock. When you pray for the prophet and obey his counsel, pay tithing with a grateful heart, and respect the sanctity of motherhood by celebrating the process of providing bodies for spirit children of God, you give your child a firm foundation on which to build. When you pray for the Holy Ghost to lead, guide, and protect, when you are faithful to your baptismal and temple covenants, when you honor marriage, and when you find solace in the scriptures and hymns, you give the child's testimony a solid bearing that Jesus Christ's "way is the path that leads to happiness in this life and eternal life in the world to come" ("The Living Christ, The Testimony of the Apostles," *Ensign,* Dec. 2004, 9).

As you do this, you show that the gospel of Jesus Christ is not an "off again, on again" experience. If the gospel is true, it is always true, in every situation and condition. You can't speak kindly to the bishop and unkindly to your husband. You can't teach that Laman and Lemuel's murmuring was sinful and then murmur yourself at the next inconvenience. Whoa, wait a minute! Is all this sounding like you have to be perfect to convey your testimony to your children? It could be perceived that way, except for the fact that if you are like I am, no matter how hard I try to live the gospel, I make mistakes every day. I think that given the fact that I do sin, my efforts to repent are the greatest evidence of my faith in the Savior and my desire to build upon His sure foundation.

In *Believing Christ,* Stephen Robinson says, "You can't make yourself perfect. You can't make yourself sinless and worthy of the presence of God the Father. You can't make yourself celestial, no matter how hard you try, because you have already sinned, and sinlessness requires not only perfect performance in the future, but also perfect performance in the past. Otherwise, you are not sinless, you are just a sinner who hasn't sinned *recently*" (28).

Brother Robinson uses the corporate analogy: "If two companies, one totally bankrupt and the other incredibly profitable, should merge to create a single, new corporation, what happens to the debts of the weaker company?" The weaker company has all the assets of the profitable company. He makes an athletic analogy: in team sports, it doesn't matter which of the players makes the points. When one individual scores, the whole team scores. "If the quarterback throws a touchdown ball to the tight end, it doesn't matter that the guards never touched the ball, or even that the defense was sitting on the bench. It doesn't matter that some on the team may have missed their blocks or run the wrong routes. It doesn't even matter that the second or third string hadn't yet been in the game" (*Believing Christ,* 28–29).

Brother Robinson shows that the incredibly profitable company is Jesus Christ. It's like having your name on His credit card. His resources are infinite. He is also the quarterback of your team. It is through His Atonement that you and I are saved and win eternal life.

As you evidence that your belief in Christ is constant in and through and around the storms of life, your children will believe and ultimately gain their own personal testimony of the Savior. It is the most joyous of days when one by one your children join you in knowing that they are under the umbrella of the Atonement. That image reverberates in my soul. I wonder if it's the image the Savior described using a mother hen and her chicks: "How often would I have gathered thy children together, even as a hen gathereth her chickens under her wings" (Matt. 23:37).

Another image used in the scriptures is of knocking and opening. My friend has an eight-year-old child who is deaf. She told me how she puzzled over an unusual behavior she observed. Several times a day she'd find this child sitting quietly inside the front door of their home. He'd sit for a while, then jump up, open the door, and act disappointed when no one was there. Finally she realized that he didn't understand how hearing people know when there was someone at the door. He had never heard the *rap, rap, rap* of knocking or the *ding dong* of a doorbell.

I see a spiritual metaphor here. Occasionally, I have heard the knocking or the doorbell of quiet revelation. I'm afraid on most such times, I've been deaf to these promptings and deaf to scriptural passages or words of the prophets. When I've listened and acted with spiritual ears—listening for the Savior's voice—I've been blessed with answers, even miracles, as was the case in Acts 12:1–16.

Luke, the author of Acts, begins the chapter by explaining that King Herod had killed the Apostle James with a sword and was determined to slay Peter also. At this point in the story, Herod had apprehended Peter and put him in prison with four guards to guard him. Herod's plan was to kill Peter as soon as the Passover was over. The night before Peter is to be killed, the Saints are gathered in prayer "without ceasing," petitioning God for Peter's deliverance. Peter is in prison, bound in chains, sleeping between two guards, while two others guard the door. Luke describes what happens next:

And, behold, the angel of the Lord came upon him, and a light shined in the prison: and he smote Peter on the side, and raised him up, saying, Arise up quickly. And his chains fell off from his hands. . . . And when Peter was come to himself, he said, Now I know of a surety, that the Lord hath sent his angel, and hath delivered me out of the hand of Herod, and from all the expectation of the people of the Jews. And when he had considered the thing, he came to the house of Mary the mother of John . . . where many were gathered together praying. And as Peter knocked at the door . . . a damsel came to hearken, named Rhoda. And when she knew Peter's voice, she opened not the gate for gladness, but ran in, and told how Peter stood before the gate. And they said unto her, Thou art mad. But she constantly affirmed that it was even so. Then said they, It is his angel. But Peter continued knocking: and when they had opened the door, and saw him, they were astonished. (vv. 7–16)

Sometimes I feel spiritually deaf because of the frenetic nature of my life. There have been times I have just needed to realize that the answer I had been praying for is before me, waiting for me to hear the knock and open the door. When I have opened the door, a miracle has filled my heart with the same astonishing reality as those who were praying in Mary's house for Peter when he was actually knocking at the door. The Savior said, "I stand at the door, and knock: if any man [or woman] hear my voice, and open the door, I will come in to him, and will sup with him, and he with me" (Rev. 3:20).

What does "hear my voice" mean? I think it means that as you read the scriptures—Old Testament, New Testament, Book of Mormon, Doctrine and Covenants, Pearl of Great Price—you will become acquainted with the sound of His voice. As you listen to general conference and read the conference edition of the *Ensign,* you will hear His voice through the testimonies of His servants, the latter-day Apostles and prophets. In Doctrine and Covenants 18:33–36, Jesus says that when you read His words it is "I, Jesus Christ, your Lord and your God, [that] have spoken it." And "you can testify that you have heard my voice." Knock at the door of the scriptures, of His servants speaking, and He will open your mind to His teachings. You have heard His voice!

To celebrate the year 2000, the First Presidency and the Quorum of the Twelve Apostles issued a document known as "The Living Christ." The Museum of Church History and Art across from Temple Square created an exhibit to celebrate the life of the Savior. The exhibit had the text to "The Living Christ" printed on a large two-sided placard. Excerpts from "The Living Christ" were placed by each painting in the exhibit as events in Jesus' life were portrayed. As a docent at the museum, I was more than excited to enter this exhibit for the first time. I went to the gallery alone. As I entered, the Spirit there overwhelmed me. I walked from painting to painting and read the excerpts from the "The Living Christ." At the halfway point in the gallery, I came to the placard whereon the text of the "The Living Christ" was printed in full. The idea came to mind that I should memorize it, which I did. The full title of the document is "The Living Christ, The Testimony of the Apostles of The Church of Jesus Christ of Latter-day Saints." After I memorized it, I used it as my own testimony. And every night for a year after I said my prayers, I repeated it in my mind to keep the memorization fresh. You can imagine what kind of a year that was for me. My testimony was renewed every night and grew exponentially. I keep a copy of "The Living Christ" in the front leaf of my large-print Bible; it fits perfectly, and I read it again and again. I hope you are familiar with it and love it as I do. The first and last paragraphs read:

> As we commemorate the birth of Jesus Christ two millennia ago, we offer our testimony of the reality of His matchless life and the infinite virtue of His great atoning sacrifice. None other has had so profound an influence upon all who have lived and will yet live upon the earth.

> We bear testimony as His duly ordained Apostles—that Jesus is the Living Christ, the immortal Son of God. He is the great King Immanuel, who stands today on the right hand of His Father. He is the light, the life, and the hope

of the world. His way is the path that leads to happiness in this life and eternal life in the world to come. God be thanked for the matchless gift of His divine Son.

The process of following and worshipping Jesus Christ is the most important work you will ever do.

POWER WITHIN

Have you ever done something, said something, or reacted to something that caused someone to question your motive? Did you shrug off the challenge with the justification, "Oh, that's just the way I am"? I have. But, hopefully, as I mature, I realize that dodging responsibility with "I can't help how I _____, that's just the way I am" is the weakest of all excuses, and that all excuses are feeble.

A college friend of mine said that in his home there was no such thing as a valid excuse. Excuses were not allowed. If he didn't get his homework done, he just didn't get it done. "The dog ate it" or "I left it at school" were unthinkable. If he was late for anything, no excuse was tolerated. He was just late. My friend said that not being allowed to make excuses taught him to assume responsibility for his actions.

Dr. C. Terry Warner, a philosophy professor at BYU, makes two points that forced me to rethink excuse making and to start listening to excuses others make. "I'm sorry I'm late; I got a phone call at the last minute and there was traffic." "I'm sorry the house isn't cleaner; the children haven't done their jobs today." "I'm not being grouchy; you are frustrating me." Dr. Warner suggests that it is not the traffic or the children. It is I. I was late. I was disorganized. I was grouchy. In relationship conflicts, he says people tend to excuse their behavior and blame the other person. In reality, he says, I make myself unhappy or grouchy, late or frustrated, and I am the one who needs to change. Otherwise, I excuse myself because "that's just the way I am."

Dr. Warner goes so far as to say that in any relationship, the fault lies within the individual. Only I can change a relationship by changing myself. I can never change you. Dr. Warner makes this confession: "Nothing in my experience has been a greater source of sadness than this discrepancy, this distance, between the person I am when I am true to what I know to be right and the person I become when I am not" (*Bonds That Make Us Free: Healing Our Relationships and Coming to Ourselves,*). His thesis is that we all have the innate knowledge to know that the excuse "That's just the way I am" is living a lie.

Is it fair, for example, to expect that everyone has the knowledge and ability to keep the commandments? Should a fifty-year-old woman who joins the Church be expected to live the Word of Wisdom as strictly as a person who is taught the doctrine from her youth? Can a person who grows up unaware that chastity is a commandment be held to the same standard of morality following baptism as a lifetime member? Should those who have a family history of immature behavior be held responsible for their childish actions? What if your father "swore like a bandit" or your grandma regularly showed her temper in angry displays? Can you be blamed if you also act that way because of their example? The truth is that we all have weaknesses, but the commandments are standards everyone, with God's help, can meet. I must be responsible for my actions.

President George Q. Cannon said: "It is true that some have greater power of resistance than others, but everyone has the power to close his heart against doubt, against darkness, against unbelief . . . against anger, against hatred, against jealousy, against malice, against envy. God has given this power unto all of us, and we can gain still greater power by calling upon Him for that which we lack. If it were not so, how could we be condemned for giving way to wrong influences?" (*Gospel Truths: Discourses and Writings of George Q. Cannon,* 1:16–17).

As has been observed, the purpose of the gospel of Jesus Christ is to make bad women good and good women better. Isaiah says that each person learns "precept upon precept; line upon line" (Isa. 28:10). I can reach a little higher and do a little better in the situations I meet if I don't feel or say, "I can't help it, that's just the way I am."

A popularly held belief suggests that genetic codes and environment determine what and who a person becomes. However, in the preface to *Bonds That Make Us Free,* Dr. Warner wrote:

> People can change fundamentally, in their hearts, and not just in their outward behavior. I have been led to this conviction partly as a result of having lived through the transformation experiences of many individuals. I say *lived through* because I had very little to do with the changes they made. They brought it about themselves. That's what has delighted me about the work I have been privileged to participate in. The possibility of overcoming very deep personal and interpersonal problems lies within the power of each of us.

President Hinckley warned: "You are a part of the great processes of God under which men and women have gone before you. All that you have of body and mind will be transmitted through you to the generations yet to come, and it is so important, so everlastingly important, my brothers and sisters, that you do not become a weak link in that chain of your generations" ("Words of the Living Prophet," *Liahona*, May 2001, 16).

Whether you think you'll never live up to your parents' graces, or that your background has irrevocably handicapped you, human nature can turn high or low expectations into an excuse. But there is no justification, no apology or excuse for passing on a troublesome characteristic or not passing on an exceptional quality to the next generation. You and I have that potential and that responsibility—to pass on the best; the power is within us.

SISTERS

Becoming a member of The Church of Jesus Christ of Latter-day Saints is for eternity. The opportunities are endless and the blessings innumerable. One of the greatest of these opportunities and blessings for a woman is to have millions of sisters. These sisters are not like the friends Lord Byron described in a letter to Mary Shelley: "I have had, and may have still, a thousand friends, as they are called in life, who are like one's partners in the waltz of this world—not much remembered when the ball is over" (as quoted in greatest-quotations.com).

My sisters in the gospel help me, teach me, and inspire me. They cry and laugh with me. They share common values and aspirations. Some of my gospel sisters are as close, and their friendship as precious, as if we were born of the same mother.

> *Oh, the comfort—the inexpressible comfort*
> *Of feeling safe with a person,*
> *Having neither to weigh thought,*
> *Nor measure words—but pouring them*
> *All right out—just as they are—*
> *Chaff and grain together—*
> *Certain that a faithful hand will*
> *Take and sift them—*
> *Keep what is worth keeping—*
> *And with the breath of kindness*
> *Blow the rest away.*
> (Dinah Maria Mulock Craik, as quoted in storybin.com)

I feel fortunate to have many friends who regularly, with the breath of kindness, blow the chaff away. These friends concentrate more on velvety petals than on thorns.

A newly married young husband, finding that marriage didn't meet his expectations, had fallen into an escalating pattern of fault-finding. He felt troubled and didn't know how to work through the friction he was feeling with his wife of a few months. One morning as he was getting ready for work, he looked in the bathroom mirror and felt as though someone were handing him a rose. He looked at its beauty, then noticed a thorn. In an instant he knew he could spend the rest of his life scorning the thorn or admiring the rose. Thorns, like chaff, are to be ignored. It's an abiding principle in all friendships.

Friends come in layers. The foundation of friendship, speaking of sisters in the gospel, is the common beliefs you and I share. Have you ever met a sister in the gospel from another state or country and within two or three sentences felt a bond? That's the sisterhood that binds millions and millions of Relief Society sisters worldwide who unite under the banner of the gospel of Jesus Christ.

Up one layer is a much smaller group—the sisters in your ward. They teach your children in Primary, and you are their visiting teachers. You serve with them on the activities committee, and your children are their children's friends. Or they may be much older or much younger; but you know each other's circumstance, greet each other in the grocery store, and trade casseroles in times of need. In ratio, there are millions in the first group and perhaps only seventy or so in this second.

At the top of the friendship pyramid are the few with whom you share a closeness that lasts even when you move from the ward. You feel commonalities. You are pushed in their presence to be a better you, not because you feel intimidated, inferior, or competitive, but because they encourage you to reach higher.

Artist David Linn painted, in blacks and whites, grays and browns, a work titled *Ascent*. It's a visual representation of "Me lift thee and thee lift me, and we both ascend together" (John Greenleaf Whittier, www.thoughtsforyou.com). The painting shows people on different steps of a rugged cement staircase. Each person is reaching down to lift the person on the stair below, and each is reaching up to take the hand of the person on the step above.

In practical, everyday life, does this mean we are all best friends? No, not at all. But it does mean you extend your hand to every sister who reaches up to you. It means no sister should ever feel excluded. It means no sister gossips or rehearses the negative. It means cliques aren't a part of Relief Society. Strong friendships? Yes! Exclusive relationships? No! Membership is open to all. Although He is not portrayed in the painting, it is the Savior who reaches down to every sister who reaches up. That's the beauty of the phrase "reaches my reaching" ("Where Can I Turn for Peace?" *Hymns*, 129). Every sister, no matter where she is on the staircase, deserves your love and prayers. If you feel there is room for growth and change in any of the above in your ward, let it begin with you. In the Whittier quote, "me lift" comes before "thee lift."

That's gospel sisterhood. As I lift, I lift not only another, but also myself. You lift, and both you and the sister you are helping climb up a step. One moment you are the lifter, and the next moment the one being lifted. In other relationships, you switch roles with any number of other sisters. Why does this work so well? It's because as we follow the example of our Heavenly Father and our Savior, who do this perfectly, I blow away your chaff and you ignore my thorns.

THE KINGDOM OF
GOD AND SMALL STONES

The book of Daniel tells about King Nebuchadnezzar, who dreamed a dream that troubled him greatly. He asked his wise men—astrologers—to tell him what the dream meant. They said, "Tell us your dream, and we will give you the interpretation." The king told them he could not remember the dream. The wise men said they could not interpret a dream he could not remember.

Living at this time was the prophet Daniel (the same Daniel who was put in a den of lions). When Daniel heard about the king's dream, he prayed and asked God to reveal the dream to him, according to His will. God showed Daniel King Nebuchadnezzar's dream, in vision. Daniel helped the king remember his dream and explained that the dream was a prophecy about the latter days. Since these are the latter days, this dream, with its interpretation, is very important.

To paraphrase, Daniel said, "In your dream you saw a stone that was cut out of the mountain without hands, which became a great mountain and filled the whole earth. The stone represents the kingdom of God that will be set up in the latter days, which shall never be destroyed. It will start out small but will roll forward, becoming larger and larger, until it fills the whole earth" (see Dan. 2).

The small stone cut out of the mountain is The Church of Jesus Christ of Latter-day Saints, or the kingdom of God on earth. I am filled with awe as I contemplate how the kingdom of God is growing and that my family and I have the privilege of living to see Daniel's prophecy being fulfilled. I knew that the Church in this dispensation started out small and that it was growing, but I didn't know to what extent until I did the research to trace the growth of the Church. When I was finished, a feeling of momentum and destiny that is great and grand, purposeful and divine, filled my soul. I hope you find these facts as amazing as I have.

(The following statistics are rounded and approximate as of year ends. For example, Joseph Smith died on June 27, 1844, but statistics for his life are stated as if he had lived to December 31, 1844. Also, a president's tenure is counted from the day the preceding prophet died rather than when he was actually ordained the President of the Church.)

- Joseph Smith served 14 years—from 1830 to 1844. He organized the Church April 6, 1830, with six official members. When he died in 1844, there were 26,000 members, the Book of Mormon was printed in one language—English; and there was one temple in Kirtland.

- Brigham Young served as Church President 33 years—from 1844 to 1877. At his death there were 115,000 members. The Book of Mormon had been translated into seven more languages—Danish, German, French, Italian, Welsh, Hawaiian, Spanish—and there had been two more temples dedicated in Nauvoo and St. George.

- John Taylor served 10 years—from 1877 to 1887. When he died in 1887, there were 173,000 members. The Book of Mormon was now available in Swedish, making a total of nine languages; and there was one additional temple in Logan.

- Wilford Woodruff served 11 years—from 1887 to 1898. At his death, Church membership had risen to 267,000. The Book of Mormon had been translated into Maori and Dutch, and the Manti and Salt Lake Temples had been dedicated.

- Lorenzo Snow served 3 years—from 1898 to 1901. In those three years, 26,000 had joined the Church to make a total membership in 1901 of 293,000. There were no additional languages or temples. (President Snow's presidency focused on leading the Church through a financial crisis. As an elderly man he traveled by horse and buggy to preach the law of tithing, which helped to resolve the burden of debt.)

- Joseph F. Smith served 17 years—from 1901 to 1918. At his death, there were 496,000 members of the Church. There were four new Book of Mormon languages (Samoan, Tahitian, Turkish, Japanese); no new temples were dedicated. (President Smith was able to bring the Church out of debt. He purchased many historic sites, preserving the heritage of the Church.)

- Heber J. Grant served 27 years—from 1918 to 1945. Membership in 1945 was 979,000. There were four new Book of Mormon languages (Czech, Armenian-Western, English Braille, Portuguese) and three new temples (Laie, Hawaii; Cardston, Alberta Canada; Mesa, Arizona).

- George Albert Smith served 6 years—from 1945 to 1951. During his presidency, the Church celebrated it first million members, and by his death Church membership had increased to 1,147,000. (It took the restored Church about 120 years to reach the first million members.) There were two new languages of the Book of Mormon—Tongan and Norwegian—and the Saints in Idaho Falls, Idaho, had a temple.

- David O. McKay served 19 years—from 1951 to 1970. In 1970 Church membership had ballooned to almost three million— 2,930,810 to be exact. Translations of the Book of Mormon in Finnish, Rarotongan, Chinese, and Korean came off the press, and five new temples were dedicated in Bern, Switzerland; Los Angeles, California; Hamilton, New Zealand; London, England; and Oakland, California.

- Joseph Fielding Smith served 2 years—from 1970 to 1972. When President Smith passed away in 1972 there were 3,219,000 members of the Church. The Book of Mormon was translated into Afrikaans, and Utah received two new temples in Ogden and Provo.

• Harold B. Lee served 18 months—from 1972 to 1973. Membership at his death was 3,307,000. There were no new languages of the Book of Mormon or temples. (President Lee's short presidency did much to organize the Church by correlating lesson manuals, procedures, and policies, which set the stage for future growth.)

• Spencer W. Kimball served 12 years—from 1973 to 1985. At his death in 1985, there were 5,919,000 members. Forty-four new translations of the Book of Mormon came into circulation, and twenty-one new temples were dedicated.

• Ezra Taft Benson served 9 years—from 1985 to 1994. In 1994 there were 9,024,000 members, 18 new translations of the Book of Mormon were completed, and nine additional temples were dedicated.

• Howard W. Hunter served 11 months—from 1994 to 1995. At his death, Church membership stood at 9,338,000, and there were two new Book of Mormon translations—American Sign Language and Spanish Braille—and two new temples in Orlando, Florida, and Bountiful, Utah.

• Gordon B. Hinckley has served since 1995. Church membership to date is more than twelve million. There have been 17 new Book of Mormon languages and 72 new temples, bringing the number to 119. (All of the preceding statistics are taken from *The Church Almanac, 2005*.) ("Dedications of the first 50 currently operating temples spanned 120 years. The next 50 dedications spanned 3 years" [lds.org].)

Elder Bruce D. Porter said:

> We rejoice to hear of temples being reared in every quarter of the earth and of far-flung nations opening their

doors to the gospel. Built upon a foundation of Apostles and prophets, the Lord's Church is being taken to the whole world by missionaries called to proclaim His word. Sometimes, perhaps, we may be inclined to see the building of the kingdom as something that takes place beyond the horizon, far away from our own branch or ward. In truth, the Church advances both by outward expansion and by inward refinement. 'For Zion must increase in beauty, and in holiness; her borders must be enlarged; her stakes must be strengthened' (D&C 82:14). We do not have to be called to serve far from home, nor do we have to hold a prominent place in the Church or in the world to build up the Lord's kingdom. We build it in our own hearts as we cultivate the Spirit of God in our lives. We build it within our families by instilling faith in our children. And we build it through the organization of the Church as we magnify our callings and share the gospel with neighbors and friends ("Building the Kingdom," *Ensign*, May 2001, 80).

In President Hinckley's conference address on October 4, 2003, he referred to the stone cut out of the mountain without hands. He said we are all ordinary people in an extraordinary cause, helping to build the Church and kingdom of God on the earth. He said the future before us can be scarcely imagined. He asked every member to be true and faithful and to work to build the kingdom. He said the Church is not a social group. It is more than meetings, even sacrament meeting, and more than attending the temple, because the Church is the kingdom of God on earth.

He said you might feel lonely as you stand for truth and goodness, but you have the forces of heaven to help you. He quoted the prophet Elisha who, though encompassed by a fearsome army on every side, said to his servant, "Fear not: for they that be with us are more than they that be with them" (2 Kgs. 6:16). Then a vision opened and the servant saw an innumerable host of heavenly warriors ready to aid the cause of righteousness. President Hinckley added the Lord's words from Doctrine and Covenants 6:36: "Look unto me in every thought; doubt not, fear not." This "marvelous work and a wonder" will fulfill its divine mandate with or without you and me. It is your privilege and mine to help fill the earth with the gospel of Jesus Christ. Mothers are the single greatest influence on missionaries, bishops, stake presidents, Apostles, prophets, home teachers, visiting teachers, Relief Society presidents, Primary children, Primary teachers, Young Women and Young Men leaders, teens, and adults; after all, every one of these individuals has a mother. Faithful Latter-day Saint mothers rock the cradles that hold the future of the Church and are the ones who are in a large part fulfilling Daniel's prophecy: "And in the days of these kings shall the God of heaven set up a kingdom, which shall never be destroyed: and the kingdom shall not be left to other people, but it shall break in pieces and consume all these kingdoms, and it shall stand for ever. Forasmuch as thou sawest that the stone was cut out of the mountain without hands, and that it brake in pieces the iron, the brass, the clay, the silver, and the gold; the great God hath made known to the king what shall come to pass hereafter: and the dream is certain, and the interpretation thereof sure" (Dan. 2:44–45).

YESTERDAY

What is your attitude about your past? Is it present with you as a negative or a positive? Do your yesterdays cast shadows on today? Do yesterday's sins produce today's guilt? Do you feel the past is past and it can't be changed? If you feel or believe any of these thoughts about the past, then perhaps you don't understand the gospel of Jesus Christ. How is that for a bold statement? The fourth article of faith states: "We believe that the first principles and ordinances of the Gospel are: first, Faith in the Lord Jesus Christ; second, Repentance; third, Baptism by immersion for the remission of sins; fourth, Laying on of hands for the gift of the Holy Ghost." Faith and repentance are prominent players in dealing with the past.

Repentance is the gift Jesus Christ has given you and me to change the past. If I don't repent, for me, it is just as though the Atonement didn't happen and Jesus suffered in Gethsemane and on the cross in vain. The doctrine of applying the blessings of the Atonement through repentance and partaking of the sacrament are magnificent, so magnificent the hymn says, "I scarce can take it in" ("How Great Thou Art," *Hymns,* 186).

Of that glorious day when Jesus personally taught the Nephites, the Book of Mormon states: "And when the disciples had done this [administered the sacrament], Jesus said unto them: Blessed are ye for this thing which ye have done, for this is fulfilling my commandments, and this doth witness unto the Father that ye are willing to do that which I have commanded you. And this shall ye always do to those who repent and are baptized in my name; and ye shall do it in remembrance of my [body and] blood, which I have shed for you, that ye may witness unto the Father that ye do always remember me. And if ye do always remember me ye shall have my Spirit to be with you" (3 Ne. 18:10–12).

The sacrament, the reason for sacrament meeting, is to renew your covenants of baptism. Your part of the covenant is to repent and be *willing* to take upon yourself the name of Christ. Jesus' part is to grant you an incomparable blessing: His Spirit to be with you.

Baptism, a once-in-a-lifetime experience, opens the gate to the kingdom of God. Jesus said, "Verily, verily, I say unto thee, Except a man be born again, he cannot see the kingdom of God" (John 3:3). The sacrament, a weekly experience, keeps that gate open, offering you the opportunity to come before the Lord, feel remorse for your sins, repent, and express your *willingness* to keep His commandments. In this way you can be washed clean every week.

There are three major requirements to this process: keep the commandments, always remember Jesus Christ, and be *willing* to take His name upon you. This is Heavenly Father's way to keep His Saints on the path toward eternal life; you and I (and every other member of the Church) need frequent reminders.

But, you are saying, there are two impossible requirements in the sacrament prayers. How can a person "always remember Him" and "always keep His commandments"? What a good question! The answer is given in the prayer on the bread. The reason you can honestly covenant to keep both these promises is because God, the Eternal Father, has, in His wisdom, provided a loophole. Perhaps you have wondered why a certain word has been italicized throughout this chapter. Listen to the word *willing* in the prayer on the bread from Doctrine and Covenants 20:77: "O God, the Eternal Father, we ask thee in the name of thy Son, Jesus Christ, to bless and sanctify this bread to the souls of all those who partake of it, that they may eat in remembrance of the body of thy Son, and witness unto thee, O God, the Eternal Father, that they are *willing* to . . ."

Stephen Robinson, in *Believing Christ*, notes:

> Why are the three words "are willing to" necessary here? Are they important? Would it make a difference if the prayer left these out and just read: "and witness unto thee,

O God, the Eternal Father, that they take upon them the name of thy Son, and always remember him and keep his commandments which he has given them"?

Yes, it would make a difference. It would make a difference because I cannot do this latter thing. I can't witness, affirm, or swear that I *do* always remember him and keep his commandments. I would be lying, and I know it—I want to do the right thing, but sometimes I don't. This is precisely the problem that makes the Atonement of Christ and the gospel covenant necessary for me in the first place—I can't keep all the commandments all the time no matter how hard I try. It follows that I can't honestly witness to God that I *will* keep all the commandments when I know that, in some degree at least, I probably won't.

However, I can with absolute honesty witness that I *am willing to*. I can swear that this is the desire of my heart. I can affirm that I hunger and thirst after these things, that I will do all I can to be obedient. Thus even by the technical terms of the covenant-renewal prayer, God lets me know that the honest commitment of my heart and my best efforts are sufficient for the covenant to be renewed, and that the covenant of faith is sufficient, through the grace of Christ, to justify me before God. (53–54)

Repentance is the miracle of evolution. Through repentance Heavenly Father heals me and changes me into a new being. Yesterday's guilt turns to testimony of and thanksgiving for Jesus Christ. Okay, repentance helps change the past, but how do I go forward? I don't like my life when I feel I'm running in place. I know that my future will 'be the same as my past unless I do things differently. I need faith to make a plan to move aggressively forward into the future. How do I prepare for the unknown of the days yet to come? By having faith in Heavenly Father. During my cancer experience I learned to stop focusing on yesterday and go forward with and in faith.

"Three weeks after your first chemotherapy treatment," my oncologist mentioned on the tail end of two hours of counsel and instruction, "your hair will fall out. I suggest you buy a wig before that first chemo treatment. You might not feel good enough afterwards." So the week before toxins were first injected into my bloodstream, I shopped for wigs, which turned out to be a difficult task. What kind of a wig did I want, something radical or a wig that looked natural? After trying on dozens of wigs in dozens of big and little stores, I knew I wanted a wig most like my natural hair so I'd feel like me. After an exhausting week of going from store to store, I found my two favorite wigs at a small shop close to home. I couldn't make a decision and called my husband and asked him to come and make the decision. I wanted to please him. He gave his opinion. I took his lead and chose the wig most like my real hair. Little did I anticipate that one of the most helpful and significant moments of my whole cancer experience, perhaps my whole life, was just about to happen.

I walked to the cash register to pay for the wig. The owner who had helped me wrote out a receipt. I saw her write a word on the receipt that I couldn't read because I didn't have my glasses with me. "What did you write?" I asked.

"I wrote the name of the wig," she responded.

"Wigs have names?" I asked.

"Yes. Most have women's names."

"What's my wig's name?" I asked.

"Faith," she answered.

So out of those twenty or so wigs I tried on, I was given Faith. "It's a message from heaven," I thought. "I will walk in Faith; I will talk in Faith; I will pray in Faith; I will think and do and be and get well in Faith." Now, eight years later, I still feel awe when I recall that moment, and I resolve again to go forward with faith in my Father in Heaven and in Jesus Christ. I think because of the cancer experience I feel differently about each day than I did before. I know to treasure today because it is all anyone has for sure. I wrote this poem to celebrate the end of 2004 and the future beyond, but mostly to celebrate today.

Past . . . Future . . . Present

The past
alas
is on the shelf
2004
all 366 days
in permanent ink
sealed
over
finished
done

The future
alas
eludes
like beams of light
'round corners
always
at least
one 90-degree twist away
unwritten
unsure
unknown

Today
the
now
milliseconds
zipping by
grasp
clutch
cling
embrace
today
the gift
called

the present
past and future
merge and hinge
on
today

SELF-BETRAYAL: LIVING A LIE

I gained more self insight from a text previously noted—*Bonds That Make Us Free.* In it I learned that "the fault lies within" each of us in troubled relationships, but (and this is the wonderful part) that the power also lies within each of us to change ourselves fundamentally. Chapter two of Warner's book is titled "Living a Lie." Is it true—am I really living a lie? If so, what can I do about it?

The chapter introduction reads:

> We are seeking to understand the source of our troubled, afflicted emotions and attitudes and the way they foul our relationships with others. Here is a clue: those times when we feel most miserable, offended, or angry are invariably the occasions when we're also most absorbed in ourselves and most anxious or suspicious or fearful, or in some other way concerned about ourselves. Why is this? Why do we get so caught up in ourselves and so ready to take offense at what others do? (19)

Dr. Warner says it's because we betray ourselves. "Self-betrayal occurs when we . . . do to another what we sense we should not do, or don't do what we sense we should. Thus self-betrayal is a sort of moral self-compromise, a violation of our own personal sense of how we ought to be and what we ought to do" (20). Another less secular approach to this phenomena is that we often ignore our conscience or the promptings of the Holy Ghost, then rationalize away the uncomfortable accompanying feeling.

Many examples are given of individuals who receive an idea of something good to do and fail to act on the prompting by reasoning it away, actually lying to themselves. Dr. Warner tells of a senior manager who feels she should say something nice to a groundskeeper, but doesn't. He rehearses the sad experience of a mother who feels she should not berate her daughter for leaving her room messy, but scolds her anyway. He tells of a father who feels he should get up with a fussy baby and let his wife sleep, but doesn't.

Joseph Smith taught that revelation from the Holy Ghost often works through such small and fleeting suggestions. "A person may profit by noticing the first intimations of the Spirit of Revelation; for instance, when you feel pure intelligence flowing unto you, it may give you sudden strokes of ideas, that by noticing it, you may find it fulfilled the same day or soon; (i.e.,) those things that were presented unto your mind by the Spirit of God, will come to pass; and thus by learning the Spirit of God and understanding it, you may grow into the principle of Revelation, until you become perfect in Christ Jesus" (Franklin D. Richards and James A. Little, *Compendium of the Doctrines of the Gospel*, 270).

Dr. Warner lists the emotions and attitudes that are red flags of self-betrayal: anger, self-pity, crustiness, suspicion, jealousy, fear, impatience, bitterness, touchiness, arrogance, boredom, discouragement, despondency, humiliation, envy, hesitancy to take initiative, resentment, contempt, indifference. He then makes a summary statement about the list:

> You will notice that these emotions and attitudes have in common some element of accusation. In addition, the list contains no attitudes or emotions that unite us with other people, but only ones that divide us from them. It includes no reference to love, delight, generosity, consideration, sympathy, or kindness. Nor does it refer to such empathetic and caring emotions and attitudes as grieving and sorrow, which are forms of emotional pain that contain no accusation. (28)

After reading chapter two of *Bonds That Make Us Free,* a busy mother (let's call her Jane) decided she would respond to all fleeting impressions to do good. She tells of the morning she awoke with the impression that she should go to the temple. She thought, *Oh, this is a prompting I can't follow. I can't leave Bob [her husband] with five children for five hours the Saturday after Christmas. There is so much to get done.* Yet she felt if she didn't respond she would be betraying herself. So she asked Bob what he thought. Would he mind if she went to the temple? (The temple was twenty miles away, but the trip took at least an hour on some of the world's busiest freeways.) Bob took his time answering. "You really think you should go? But you hate the freeways. Well, if you feel impressed . . . But I worry about your safety. At least find someone to go with you." As he said, "Find someone to go with you," one of the women Jane visit taught came to mind.

She called the woman and received a grateful response. The woman said that she was too old to brave the freeways, and no one ever invited her to go to the temple. She had recently renewed her recommend with a prayer that somehow she would be able to go.

As Jane was getting ready, the idea came that although she and her partner had visited the four women assigned to them and had taken them Christmas goodies, they hadn't given the lesson. It had been her companion's turn, and somehow it just hadn't happened. The lesson would give her something to talk about as they made their way to the temple. She grabbed the December *Ensign* and turned to the visiting teaching message. When she read the title and the last paragraph, her involuntary gasp of amazement caught her husband's attention. "What's wrong?" he asked.

"Nothing's wrong," she said. "Everything's right. The title of this month's visiting teaching message is 'Rejoice in the Blessings of the Temple,' and the last paragraph asks: 'How is our Christmas celebration made more meaningful through our knowledge of temple blessings?'"

As it turned out, Bob took the children to a movie with passes that expired in three days and got the house nearly ready for Sunday. The freeways were relatively empty, and Jane got home in four hours.

Dr. Warner sums up the concept of living a lie. "Our *undistorted* sense of right and wrong calls us to do right toward others, to act as love dictates. Most fundamentally, we are beings bonded to one another by love. In self-betrayal we violate these bonds, deceive ourselves about who we really are, harden ourselves to what we feel is right, and live a lie. Our living connection with others calls us to let go of this lie and be who we really are" (ibid., 36).

MAD?
DON'T GET MAD—TEACH

(The following stories are a result of two times when my husband set a good example for me and our children. I use these examples hesitantly because you might think that problems in our family were always handled this well. To put your mind at ease, they weren't. My husband is good, but not perfect.)

Our son Mike and his wife Shonna had been out on a date and didn't get home until late. At the time, they were parents of three children—Sarah, age five, Joshua, newly three, and Abby, a marvel at eighteen months. By the time Shonna took the babysitter home (I like this; if it's a female babysitter, Shonna takes her home), tidied up a bit, and made sure the children's Sunday clothes were assembled, it was nearly midnight. Meanwhile, Mike was adding the final touches to his Primary lesson. All was prepared for the next morning's church meetings, which began at nine o'clock.

About 6:30 Sunday morning, Sarah, in her obedient, proper, oldest-child way, stood by her mother's side of the bed and whispered, "Mommy, may I make myself a peanut butter and jam sandwich?" Shonna, without lifting an eyelid, nodded. At 6:35, Sarah was back at her mother's bedside with an unopened warehouse-size jar of jam. "Mommy, will you open the jam jar, please?" Shonna obliged. At 6:45 Sarah was again at Shonna's side of the bed. "Mommy, Mommy, I think you'd better come." Shonna, sensing major urgency in Sarah's voice, followed her downstairs to the kitchen. When she looked into the kitchen, she stopped dead in her tracks and called, "Mike!"

Mike was out of bed and down the stairs in an instant, expecting to see blood, flood, or fire. He took one look at the situation and said sternly, "Nobody move!" as he went to the hall closet and got his camera. The image saved for posterity is of Joshua and Abby sitting on the kitchen table with the half-empty raspberry jam jar between them. Both had been dipping their arms in the jar and then shaking their hands. After snapping the photo, Mike picked up Abby and carried her to a corner of the room. Putting her down, he said, "Abby, you are in time-out. You know we don't make messes with food."

Then he picked up Joshua and set him down in another corner of the room. "Joshua, you are in time-out. You are three, and three-year-olds don't play with food. You need to set a good example for Abby."

Then he took Sarah by the hand and put her in the third corner of the room. "Sarah," he said, "you are in time-out because you left the lid off the jam jar."

He then took Shonna by the hand and said, "And Daddy and Mommy are in time-out. Mommy shouldn't have opened the jam jar, and I should have gotten up with Sarah in the first place. But our time-out won't be sitting in a corner. We have to clean it up, and all of you have to watch us until we are through." Mike and Shonna cleaned the table, the floor, and the blinds and left Abby and Joshua in their stickiness. The cleanup took about an hour and a half. When finally it was time to run the bath water, two very repentant and very cute children were soaped and scrubbed, but it took several more baths on subsequent days to remove the evidence of raspberry-toned skin.

As in this example, parents can't foresee when their parenting skills will be taxed or when a teaching moment will dawn. Such opportunities seem always to happen at inconvenient times when the parent is tired or when it's late or early or when the parent is preoccupied or sleeping or working or already late for an appointment. And usually at the moment, parents are in little humor to think clearly enough to know how to discipline appropriately, let alone seize the moment to teach. And certainly it is naïve to think that all moments of crisis in the life of a family can make the photo album! But the teaching is always going to happen, no matter how you react. Whether you become angry, scream, swear, rant and rave, accuse, find fault, threaten, or resist all those tendencies and say to yourself, "Don't get mad, teach," the impressions will etch themselves indelibly in the memory and will be replicated in future generations. (Your children will respond to their children and their children to their children as you respond to them.)

Our oldest daughter, Michelle, wrote an article when she was sixteen that was published in the *New Era,* It was part of a series of articles titled "My Family." Michelle wrote:

> Luck is a marvelous thing. I know. It kept me out of a number of scrapes when I was a beginning driver of a big car.
>
> My greatest challenge was maneuvering in our two-car driveway, especially when the other car had been parked too close to the center. Then I was faced with the white Oldsmobile on one side and a one-foot concrete retaining wall on the other.
>
> Usually luck was on my side of the driveway, but one Saturday morning it just didn't hold out. As my sister and I drove up the sloping hill into the driveway, we heard a grinding noise not unlike that of a demolition crew at work.
>
> "Stop, Michelle!" Anne screamed. "You've hit the wall!"
>
> "I have not!" I insisted, but I put my foot on the brake. The grinding stopped.
>
> "Okay, Anne, so maybe I nicked the wall, but all I need to do is pull forward and . . ."
>
> The car didn't move. The back left wheel scraped itself into a spin, but the car didn't move.
>
> "Stop! I'm going to get Dad."
>
> "Don't you dare. If I can't go forward, I can always go backward . . ."

Fortunately for Anne, me, and the wall, I didn't have a chance to shift into reverse. With a sudden thrust, the back wheel spun free and the scraping stopped.

"I'm going to tell Dad." She hopped out of the car and ran into the house.

Surveying the damage, I had to admit that a demolition crew could not have done a better job. The one-foot wall had been reduced to a half-foot mound of concrete Legos.

As I walked slowly up the stairs to the front door, I remembered what was now the second worst disaster of my life. Anne was a baby then; Matt, Mike, and I were six, three, and five. We three older children were playing in the boys' bedroom when we decided to go sailing. Three empty dresser drawers made great boats, but the carpet around them looked like a still blue lake, and we wanted a stormy ocean. Soon the floor was covered with toy, clothing, and blanket waves. We were deep-sea fishing when we noticed Dad standing in the doorway. He didn't say a word. It was our worst mess ever, and he didn't say a word. He simply started to help us put our waves away.

That was 12 years ago, I reminded myself. But there Dad stood in the front doorway. He was holding a garbage can, a push broom, and a dustpan. "Uh, Dad . . ." I began. He didn't say a word. It was my worst mess ever, and he didn't say a word. He must have understood that right then I needed acceptance more than condemnation; I had already condemned myself. He just handed me the broom, and together we went down to the driveway (Michelle Linford, "My Worst Mess Ever," March 1987, 9).

Is it possible that Mike, Michelle's younger brother, recalled how their father had reacted to the stormy ocean when he was three or the retaining-wall disaster when he was fourteen? Could that be the reason that, as an adult, he resolved the raspberry jam incident in such an appropriate way? It's very, very probable. Mike and Michelle both learned from the example, and both now parent their own children that way. (In allowing me to use their stories, they both asked that I add the qualification that they are not by any means perfect parents. But who is?)

I can hear you groaning because perhaps you weren't raised that way. It's possible that when things went wrong, they *really* went wrong—yelling, swearing, blaming, or worse were the norm. If this was the case in your family, is there no hope for you as a parent? Yes. Absolutely YES! Though you may or may not have had such an example as a child, you can make sure that your children do. It makes living so much easier. Don't get mad, teach.

REVERENCE

President Spencer W. Kimball said, "We must remember that reverence is not a somber, temporary behavior that we adopt on Sunday. True reverence involves happiness, as well as love, respect, gratitude, and godly fear. It is a virtue that should be part of our way of life. In fact, Latter-day Saints should be the most reverent people in all the earth. . . . We cannot foresee the great spiritual impact on our own families if we become the reverent people we know we should be" (*The Teachings of Spencer W. Kimball*, 223–24).

President Marion G. Romney clarified why members of the Church should be the most reverent. "We should love God more than anyone else loves him because we know so much more about him" ("Reverence," *Ensign,* Sep. 1982, 3). That is the first reason to be reverent—because we love God. But reverence isn't about *we,* it's about *me.* Reverence is personal. Reverence is the outward expression of an individual's testimony, and as such, measures the individual's spiritual maturity and understanding of God and His creations. Reverence is a form of worship.

The second reason for reverence is that irreverence limits spiritual impressions. President Boyd K. Packer said, "Foyers are built into our chapels to allow for the greeting and chatter that are typical of people who love one another. However, when we step into the chapel, we must—each of us must—watch ourselves lest we be guilty of intruding when someone is struggling to feel delicate spiritual communications" (*Things of the Soul,* 92). President David O. McKay told the story of several hundred missionaries who went into the Sacred Grove for a meeting. He wished everyone in the Church could experience the quiet attitude of reverence and respect that was there. He said that even after the closing prayer, the missionaries walked out in profound silence. There was no talking or shaking of hands until they were outside the grove (see *Gospel Ideals,* 223). The missionaries didn't want to diminish the impact of such a reverent, spiritual experience. President Kimball said, "Receiving personal revelation is not a passive process. As we seek such revelations, we must prepare for these sacred experiences. . . . God reveals himself to [people] who are prepared for such manifestations" (in *Conference Report,* Apr. 1964, 97). Reverence is a necessary preparation to feeling the Spirit.

Home is the best place to learn and practice reverence. Parents, often the mother, must look for ways and opportunities to help children experience the quiet reverence that allows the Spirit to teach. An early morning hike, watching a sunrise or sunset, singing Primary songs and hymns, reading scriptures, observing a sleeping baby, and kneeling together can be reverent moments to share. Significant family events such as births, deaths, baptisms, and weddings provide opportunities to talk about reverence for Heavenly Father, Jesus, and the Holy Ghost. Other sacred moments can occur when a family member is ill and requests a priesthood blessing or when a family member asks for a father's blessing prior to a new school year, or mission, or for any other reason. Speaking reverently of testimonies around the dinner table following fast and testimony meeting, anticipating and fully participating in general conferences, and prayerfully preparing for talks and lessons are other ways mothers can model reverence. Mothers teach reverence, model reverence, and create situations where the Spirit will feel comfortable; but as you know so well, you cannot *make* a child feel or be reverent. Being quiet is a good first step that you can try to enforce, but true reverence isn't transferable. True reverence is profoundly personal.

Sacrament meeting provides a weekly opportunity to be reverent. I like to watch mothers who help children under the age of four with supplements to the sacrament meeting experience, such as nonmessy food and quiet-books. It is never too early, however, to help the child listen and learn, appreciate, and seek to feel the Spirit of the sacrament meeting. Regular conversations following church about the talks or the beautiful music or the missionary's testimony in a foreign tongue, along with regular sharing of sacred thoughts that came during the sacrament, all help a child grow in reverence. Helpful are a parent's comments such as "I liked the bishop's story about . . ." or "I noticed Brother Smith reading his scriptures during the sacrament" or "Kevin Jones must have memorized many hymns. I always see him singing as he breaks the bread at the sacrament table." Other reverent attitudes such as not leaving early, not minding if the meeting lasts a little longer than scheduled, arriving on time, singing the hymns, not littering, caring for Church property, and visiting outside the chapel are some of the many ways you and I can show reverence. Reverence is a measure of love for God and evidence of a profound desire to feel the presence of His Spirit.

FORGOING:
A LIFE-ALTERING PRINCIPLE

In the last chapter of the book *Bonds That Make Us Free,* Dr. C.
Terry Warner explains a principle he calls "forgoing." He defines
forgoing as the purposeful act of overlooking or allowing a grievance
to pass without comment or notice. It is "the daily manner of life of
those free people who don't have to spend all their time suffering
from, agonizing over, and repenting of their repeated mistakes" (302).

Dr. Warner writes: "Forgoing the taking of offense is an achievement of the one who forgoes. . . . [It is a gift] he or she extends . . .
to all including those nearest by. It cannot depend upon what others
do, or else it is not genuine forgoing." And he warns, "Unless we
change in our hearts toward the people we struggle with here and
now, we are condemned to struggle with whomever we may find
ourselves associating with. . . . It doesn't matter if we marry a
different spouse, take another job, or move to another country. We
will be the same; we will interpret our world the same way, and
others will respond to us the same ways. The details of our days may
distinguish them from one another, but their substance will not
change. 'Wherever you go, there you are.' Nothing can change
fundamentally until we change fundamentally" (ibid., 307). The
principle of forgoing works because if I change, you cannot respond
to me as you did before, because the "old me" no longer exists. You
must respond to me in another way. Forgoing works independently
of what the other person does or does not do.

Forgoing is more than just not saying something about the irritation; it's more than having the discipline to let the irritation pass
seemingly unnoticed. When I forgo, I don't have to control my

response because I am honestly not irritated or angry or insulted. I am free of all those negative feelings. What kinds of situations call for the act of forgoing? Everything that triggers the following scenario: Something happens, and if I respond to it in my "natural woman" way, I would allow myself to become angry, miffed, or insulted; to think or act sarcastically; to sulk, name-call, accuse, or berate; to give the silent treatment to; to try to make you, the other, feel guilty; to feel self-pity; or to play the martyr.

Here is an example. Bill, a good husband and father, has an idiosyncrasy or two. One is that it drives him crazy to see a book left open and facedown. Laura, his wife, and his children know well of this quirk. They think it is unnecessarily meticulous. But they don't want to upset him and hear the lecture about the fragile nature of bookbindings. So they usually find a bookmark to mark the page, unless they think he won't notice or won't come home before they finish reading.

Laura loves to read at night before Bill comes to bed. This night she is very sleepy, decides to stop reading, and puts her book facedown on the nightstand beside the bed. She knows it will irritate Bill, but she rationalizes that his obsession about book care is one of several weird ways he tries to control her. She decides she won't be controlled in this way, when she suddenly remembers that she just read about forgoing. She's too tired to get up to find a bookmark so she turns over and closes the book with a promise to herself that she will never put a book facedown again. Bill comes to bed and never knows about the little sacrifice his wife just made for him. But over the course of the next few months, Bill notices that Laura is different. Living with her seems to be easier in some indefinable way. He likes it.

One night he comes to bed to see that Laura has fallen asleep while reading. The book has fallen out of her hands and is facedown on the blanket! His first impulse is to wake her up and remind her about the care of books, but somehow it just doesn't seem to matter as much as it has in the past. Without knowing the name for what he is doing, Bill forgoes. When Laura awakes, she fears that she may have fallen asleep without taking proper care of the book. She looks around the bed and then sees it on the nightstand. She wonders, *Did I put it there or did Bill?* She thinks it was Bill. She feels loved.

Does forgoing work with big, bad problems as well? Dr. Warner gives this example. Melinda's husband kept "his secretary in a nearby apartment, had a baby by her, attended the birth, named the baby after himself, and put a birth announcement in the newspaper!" When it became obvious that reconciliation was impossible, Melinda "accepted the circumstance without resentment and concentrated upon this point: if she and her husband were to part because of his refusal to make a marriage with her, and she left without resentment or recrimination, she would be able to leave and live freely. Otherwise, she would remain tied to him by bonds of anguish even if he were to move to the other side of the world. . . . She emerged a person completely free of self-pity, loving her life. She obtained an advanced degree and became a counselor" (ibid., 309).

I have told many people about the principle of forgoing. I even used it in a talk at an enrichment night. A woman took me on and said forgoing meant relinquishing, giving up. I agreed with her. She said I didn't understand. I thought she didn't understand. She said that if she practiced forgoing in her life, she would be swallowed up and trodden on. She said forgoing is a principle for ostriches who put their heads in the sand and pretend that bad situations don't exist. I tried to explain that when a woman forgoes, she still takes care of business, whatever that necessitates, but that forgoing works independently of whatever others do. I tried to explain that the forgoing comes in relinquishing and giving up the accompanying anger and unforgiving attitude toward the one who offends or in giving up a behavior that creates such conflict in another. In one of the previous examples, Laura forwent the annoyance she could have felt toward her husband, making her free of that emotional baggage; what she did with the book was not the point as much as what that action represented and what it freed her from feeling. That's how forgoing works with minor problems. Melinda, on the other hand, had a major problem. Did she put her head in the sand? No. She took care of business and chose to be in a healthier environment; she divorced her husband and got on with life. The beautiful part of her story is that through forgoing she was able to let the anger and harboring of ill will go, making her free of those chains. Forgoing is a true principle because it is a manifestation of charity. You can know if it is true for yourself by trying it. Jesus said, "If any man will do his will, he shall know of the doctrine, whether it be of God, or whether I speak of myself" (John 7:17). Look over and beyond the next offense. Don't keep track of offenses; don't revisit them; just let them go, and your life will change in ways you cannot foresee. Marriages have been saved; rebellious children have been reclaimed; contentious and competitive relationships have become peaceful; and hearts have been softened and opened to spiritual promptings as never before.

MURMURING:
TO DO OR NOT TO DO

Kermit the Frog on *Sesame Street* sang, "It's not easy being green."
Well, Kermit, it's not easy being anything. It's not easy being
young or old. It's not easy being male or female. And sometimes
when it's especially not easy, we sing a mournful tune, as Kermit did,
spelling out our troubles and woes.

A husband calls his wife during his lunch break just to say, "I love
you. Hope you're having a good day." The wife and busy mother tells
him the "news" of the morning. "Amy couldn't find her math assignment, which caused her to miss the bus. So I raced around to help her
find it and fell over your gardening shoes you left in the hall, nearly
spraining my ankle. I grabbed the baby and Jared and hobbled to the
car to take her to school. When I opened the door to the van, a
horrid smell greeted us. I think one of your Scouts left something
dead under the seat after your campout, so I opened the windows.
On the way the baby threw up, and Jared got out of his car seat and
threw one of his shoes out the window. I was so distracted by all this I
didn't notice a radar trap and got a ticket for going more than twenty
miles an hour in a school zone, and the policeman was the bishop!"
What part of this monologue is the "news" of the morning and what
is murmuring?

In the *Guide to the Scriptures*, the volume that combines the
Topical Guide and the Bible Dictionary in languages other than
English (lds.org), *murmur* is defined: "to grumble and complain
against God's purposes, plans, or servants." Some dictionaries define a
murmur as "an indistinct complaint." In the exaggerated story above,
is the wife murmuring? Does she need to repent?

Exodus 15:23–16:3 tells about the murmuring of the children of Israel. Moses declared, "For that the Lord heareth your murmurings which ye murmur against him: . . . your murmurings are not against us, but against the Lord" (16:8).

Laman and Lemuel are infamous Book of Mormon murmurers. "And thus, Laman and Lemuel . . . did murmur against their father. And they did murmur because they knew not the dealings of that God who had created them" (1 Ne. 2:12).

In the time of Christ, the Apostle John records that Jesus said, "Murmur not among yourselves" (John 6:43).

In the early history of the Church in this dispensation, the Lord told Oliver Cowdery: "Do not murmur, my son, for it is wisdom in me that I have dealt with you after this manner" (D&C 9:6). Emma Smith was cautioned: "Murmur not because of the things which thou hast not seen, for they are withheld from thee and from the world, which is wisdom in me in a time to come" (D&C 25:4). Joseph Smith said, "Remember not to murmur. . . . You are not as yet brought into as trying circumstances as were the ancient Prophets and Apostles. Call to mind Daniel, the three Hebrew children, Jeremiah, Paul, Stephen . . . who were stoned, sawn asunder, tempted, slain with a sword, and wandered about in sheep skins . . . destitute, afflicted, tormented" (*History of the Church*, 1:450). George A. Smith reported that the Prophet Joseph told him "that I should never get discouraged, whatever difficulties might surround me. If I were sunk into the lowest pit of Nova Scotia and all the Rocky Mountains piled on top of me, I ought not to be discouraged, but hang on, exercise faith, and keep up good courage, and I should come out on the top of the heap" (Zora Smith Jarvis, comp., *Ancestry, Biography, and Family of George A. Smith*, 54).

Several years after the pioneers arrived in the Salt Lake Valley, Brigham Young spoke to a group of workmen and their wives at a Christmas celebration. Because of storms, these workers had not been able to finish the roof on the adobe Tabernacle on the temple block where the celebration had been planned. The party was held in an adjoining carpenter's shop, and there was some grumbling. On this occasion, President Young said:

Five years ago we were menaced on every side by the cruel persecutions of our inveterate enemies; hundreds of families who had been forced from their homes, and compelled to leave behind them their all, were wandering as exiles in a state of abject destitution; but by the favor of heaven, we have been enabled to surmount all these difficulties and can assemble here today, in the chamber of these mountains, where there is none to make us afraid, far from our persecutors, far from the turmoil and confusion of the old world. Brethren and sisters, has not the Lord poured out his blessings upon you to surpass all former times? Your barns and your presses are filled with fine wheat, and other products in these valleys; your tables groan under the abundance of the blessings of the Almighty. Is there room for one complaint or murmur by this people? No! You are full with the blessings of God; you can sit down and eat and drink until you are satisfied. There are hundreds of thousands in the old world who can say, they never did have enough to satisfy the cravings of nature. There are thousands at this time who would crawl upon their hands and knees, or travel on foot over the mighty ocean, were there a highway cast up, carrying their little children upon their backs, to obtain the blessings that we this day enjoy. That day of peace and plenty which the Saints have looked for from the commencement of this Church, has in a great measure come to pass. (Preston Nibley, *Brigham Young: The Man and His Work,* 169)

So it is today. It's not easy, but even in the best of circumstances those prone to murmuring will find things to grumble about. President Hinckley in discussing God's admonition to Emma Smith to "murmur not" said:

I believe he [the Lord] is saying to each of us, be happy. The gospel is a thing of joy. It provides us with a reason for gladness. Of course there are times of sorrow. Of course there are hours of concern and anxiety. We all worry. But the

Lord has told us to lift our hearts and rejoice. I see so many people, including many women, who seem never to see the sunshine, but who constantly walk with storms under cloudy skies. Cultivate an attitude of happiness. Cultivate a spirit of optimism. Walk with faith, rejoicing in the beauties of nature, in the goodness of those you love, in the testimony which you carry in your heart concerning things divine. ("'If Thou Art Faithful,'" *Ensign,* Nov. 1984, 92)

What is the difference between recounting facts, expressing feelings, and murmuring? It may be a fine line, but the Spirit knows when you are murmuring. If you are thinking of saying something that is borderline murmuring, just don't say it. I have felt the Spirit literally leap from me when I have begun to murmur. In those dramatic moments, I've tried to redirect my thoughts midsentence and reframe the words so that I wouldn't murmur. I know I must repent if I grumble and complain against God's purposes, plans, or servants.

The absolute greatest example of not murmuring is the Savior of this world. He is the supreme example of all nonmurmurers, even on the cross. We can also look to the prophets as great examples in this area. If Joseph Smith and Brigham Young had been murmurers, they would have had sufficient material to fill volumes with their discontent. But they didn't, and neither does President Hinckley. I am working on following his admonition to "cultivate a spirit of optimism" and murmur not.

OBEDIENCE

Afamily decided to drive two hundred miles and cut a real Christmas tree in a real forest. Two weeks before Christmas, the entire family, including two married children and their families who also wanted "real" trees, set off on the great Christmas-tree hunt with chain saws and trailer in tow. When they arrived at the last town before the forest, they pulled into the gas station and the father asked the attendant where the best place was to cut Christmas trees. "Well, what does your permit say?"

"Permit? I need a permit?"

"Yeah, you get them at the courthouse at the county seat."

The father looked at his watch. It was 4:00 P.M. and over an hour's drive back to the county seat. "Do you know what time they close?" the father asked.

"I think they shut down at 4:30," was the response.

The father chose not to get the permit. He drove into the forest and cut down three trees as quickly as possible. In retelling the story, the father said the whole time they were cutting down the trees, he kept looking over his shoulder for the park ranger, and even though the trees were most beautiful, he'd never enjoyed a Christmas tree less. He said the tree was fresh and lasted well into January, and every time the doorbell rang, he expected to see the posse who had come to take him to jail. The Lord has admonished, "Let no man break the laws of the land, for he that keepeth the laws of God hath no need to break the laws of the land" (D&C 58:21). When you obey, you don't have to continually look over your shoulder or watch your back; you don't need a superb memory to cover a trail of lies. You can look others straight in the eye. Obeying the law makes you free. "And ye shall know the truth, and the truth shall make you free" (John 8:32). When you know the truth and do the truth, you are free. Free from what? Free from the consequences that result from disobedience.

In the scriptures, the image of chains and binding is often used: "Yea, and he [the devil] leadeth them by the neck with a flaxen cord, until he bindeth them with his strong cords forever" (2 Ne. 26:22). "O that ye would awake; awake from a deep sleep, yea, even from the sleep of hell, and shake off the awful chains by which ye are bound, which are the chains which bind the children of men, that they are carried away captive down to the eternal gulf of misery and woe" (2 Ne. 1:13). "O, my beloved brethren, turn away from your sins; shake off the chains of him that would bind you fast" (2 Ne. 9:45). You "must needs be stirred up unto repentance, or the devil will grasp [you] with his everlasting chains" (2 Ne. 28:19).

Nephi explains how the devil slips his chains around his victims seemingly thread by thread before we realize to whose voice we are hearkening. How does he do it? First, he flatters us. Then, when he has our prideful attention, he preaches false doctrine, whispering, "there is no hell. . . . I am no devil, for there is none." Soon "his awful chains, from whence there is no deliverance" have snared another prisoner (2 Ne. 28:22).

Alma says these chains of hell are like a "deep sleep," like being in "the midst of darkness" such that you are "encircled about by the bands of death." He says the consequence of listening to Satan is "an everlasting destruction" (Alma 5:7). Speaking to the people of Ammonihah regarding the apostate Zeezrom, Alma says, "And behold I say unto you all that this was a snare of the adversary, which he has laid to catch this people, that he might bring you into subjection unto him, that he might encircle you about with his chains, that he might chain you down to everlasting destruction, according to the power of his captivity" (Alma 12:6). He warns that those who harden their hearts suffer spiritual malnutrition. As they listen to Satan, "to them is given the lesser portion of the word until they know nothing concerning [God's] mysteries." And as their knowledge decreases, the control of Satan increases until "they are taken captive by the devil, and led by his will down to destruction. Now this is what is meant by the chains of hell" (Alma 12:11). Obedience is the only way you or I can be free. Obeying the laws of the land is important and probably causes more consternation than breaking the laws of God, because the punishment for violating the laws of the land happens here and now. Those without faith in Jesus Christ probably don't worry much about breaking the laws of God. The fact is, however, if I disobey the laws of the land, I am breaking God's law at the same time. And God's judgments will occur. Mercy can never rob justice because obedience is the first law of heaven.

In the early days of the Church there was some disagreement over what the first law of heaven was. Some said it was order; others said it was obedience. President Joseph F. Smith in 1896 answered the question:

> It is frequently said that order is the first law of heaven. I wish to put this in a different light. Order in the Church is the result of obedience to the laws of God and to the discipline which He has established among men. My opinion is that obedience, which one of the ancient prophets said was "better than sacrifice," is the first law of heaven—if there can be any law called the first or above all others. Without obedience there can be no order, no discipline, no government. The will of God cannot be done, either in the heavens or on the earth, except men will obey the will of the Father. And when men obey the will of the Father, order is the result. Confusion ceases, and peace is made to prevail, when men yield obedience to the requirements of the Father, or to the laws of God. Discipline is that practice which is necessary to bring men and women into an understanding of the laws and requirements of God; or, it is that condition which will exist when men understand the laws of God and yield obedience to them. (Brian H. Stuy, ed., *Collected Discourses,* v. 4)

Article of Faith number three proclaims: "We believe that through the Atonement of Christ, all mankind may be saved, by *obedience* to the laws and ordinances of the Gospel" (emphasis added). To Jeremiah the Lord said, "But this thing commanded I them, saying, Obey my voice, and I will be your God, and ye shall be my people: and walk ye in all the ways that I have commanded you, that it may be well unto you" (Jer. 7:23). So, obedience is the first law of heaven. I will be saved by my obedience. If I obey His voice, He will be my God. Elder Bruce R. McConkie said, "Obedience is the first law of heaven. All progression, all perfection, all salvation, all godliness, all that is right and just and true, all good things come to those who live the laws of Him who is Eternal. There is nothing in all eternity more important than to keep the commandments of God (*The Promised Messiah: The First Coming of Christ*, 126).

But am I obedient? If my obedience were graphed, would I see a flat line or an upward or downward slope? While I was pondering obedience and how obedient I really am, I read an article about a woman who wanted nothing more than to establish a relationship with Heavenly Father. I wondered about whether obedience or trying to establish a relationship with God was more important. This notion of a relationship with Deity is a common thread in talks and religious conversations in the Church. I suspect that it might be related to the Protestant view—among others—because there are frequent articles in Protestant publications about having a relationship with Jesus (I read about it at my hairdresser's). In thinking about how crucial obedience is, I thought, *What right do I have to try to establish a relationship with a God? Heavenly Father and Jesus Christ want my obedience. They set the terms of our relationship. They have everything to offer me, but I have nothing but my willing obedience to give them.* Just then, I saw a bug crawling across the floor and thought, *It's probably the same dynamic as that bug wanting a relationship with me. God's ways are not my ways.* Then I read a statement by Elder Neal A. Maxwell:

> God loves us all—saint and sinner alike—with a perfect
> and everlasting love. We have His love, if not His approval.
> It is our love for Him that remains to be developed. When
> we come to be genuinely concerned with pleasing God—
> more than with pleasing any in the world, even ourselves—
> then our behavior improves and His blessings can engulf
> us. This sublime feeling can be experienced only if we

come to know enough about Him so that our awe melts into adoration, and our respect into utter reverence. . . .

To those who mean well but thoughtlessly speak of 'building a better relationship' with God (which sounds like a transaction between mortals desiring reciprocity), it needs to be said that our relationship with God is already established, in a genealogical sense. Perhaps what such individuals intend to say is that we must draw closer to God. But we are to worship, to adore, and to obey God, not build a better relationship with Him! (*All These Things Shall Give Thee Experience*, 3)

Obedience to the laws and principles of the gospel is the way God the Eternal Father and His Son Jesus Christ are worshipped and honored; obedience is Their gauge of knowing who loves Them and who doesn't. Obedience is like a contract. When I obey God's laws, He blesses me in the here and now. I am happier, more successful, and able to live life with inner peace, which is a great reward. But He also promises greater things than this world can offer. "Eye hath not seen, nor ear heard, neither have entered into the heart of man, the things which God hath prepared for them that love him" (1 Cor. 2:9). And how do you show love to God? By obeying Him, of course. Obedience is a very good deal.

TEMPLES AND TEMPLATES

I searched "temple" on the Internet and discovered that the very first use of the word *temple* in the Old Testament is in 1 Samuel 1:9. It's the story of Hannah going to the temple to ask the Lord for a child. I think there's a message here about the value of temples in women's lives.

The word *temple* likely comes from the word *template*, meaning pattern (see *American Heritage Dictionary* [Houghton Mifflin Co.: 1975], 1325). If I lay—superimpose—a template of the temple over my life, what do I find? Order: Is my life orderly? Cleanliness: Is my life clean? Are my surroundings clean? Reverence: Am I reverent in thought, word, action, dress? True doctrine: Am I learning true doctrine? The presence of the Spirit: Do I seek the Spirit? Prayer: Do I understand prayer? Service: Do I give service? "The temple is the house of God, a place of love and beauty" ("I Love to See the Temple," *Children's Songbook,* 95). Do I seek love and beauty? The temple is a pattern, a guide to prepare me for day-to-day and eternal living.

The temple provides an opportunity to learn, commune, covenant, be sealed, and reflect upon spiritual matters, especially when we return often. My temple goal for the first thirty or so years of marriage was to do twelve endowment sessions a year. It was hard to meet that goal. Sometimes when Richard and I got to the temple, we'd do two sessions back-to-back to optimize babysitters, etc. It never occurred to me that I would ever want to go more than once a month.

One Sunday in Gospel Doctrine class, the teacher, an attorney, was teaching the book of Ezra in the Old Testament, and this particular day the topic was temples. His classes were intellectually challenging and very fun and thought-provoking, as he used his wit and glibness to interact with class members. As he was pursuing the lesson in the way to which the class had become accustomed, he put his Bible down and started telling us about his feelings for the temple.

He said that about a year previous, he was on his way to play tennis, as he did weekly, when the thought came to him, "If you can play tennis once a week, you can get to the temple once a week." Since that day, he has been in the temple once a week. Then a most improbable thing happened. The teacher began to cry as he told what a difference the temple was making in his life. What started out as a little eye dabbing turned into unabashed weeping as he said, "I can't tell you how, but attending the temple once a week makes everything in life better."

This was a revelation to me! Once a month seemed impossible, yet this man was going once a week! I kept struggling, however, to get to the temple once a month. A few years later when my children were all in school, my parents, who had been temple workers, were released. My mother told me how much she missed being in the temple and asked me if I'd ever like to go with my father and her. She suggested once a week. We compared our schedules and found that we could go every Tuesday afternoon, which we did for about six months until my father became ill. Then I stopped going weekly and went back to my once-a-month goal. But within weeks, I felt a deep hunger for the temple; so I started going by myself on Tuesday afternoons. I've learned that what my Gospel Doctrine teacher said is true; I can't tell you how, but attending the temple once a week makes everything in life better.

I am striving to make the temple the template for my life. I have the luxury of living between two temples, twenty-five minutes either to the south or to the north. As I am driving north to the temple and first see the spires of the Salt Lake Temple or as I am driving south and see Moroni glistening atop the spire of the Jordan River Temple, I sing the Primary song to myself, changing one word: "I love to see the temple. I'm going there *today*, To feel the Holy Spirit, To listen and to pray" ("I Love to See the Temple," *Children's Songbook*, 95).

PATIENCE:
NOT OPTIONAL ONCE YOU
HAVE CHILDREN

In the November 1986 *Parents Magazine,* editor-in-chief Elizabeth Crow wrote about patience. She said that patience is a virtue every parent must acquire. "Virtues are discretionary; you can choose to practice them or not. Unfortunately, however, patience is not optional once you have children." That quote could have been written a thousand years ago or today. Did your grandmother need patience? Did her mother need patience? Did mothers need patience in Book of Mormon times, New Testament times, Old Testament times? Yes, from the time Adam and Eve had their first child, parents have needed patience.

The words that most usually precede patience indicate that patience is an ongoing pursuit—*practice* patience, *exercise* patience, *develop* patience, *learn* patience. Another word that is often coupled with patience is *long-suffering.* What does long-suffering mean? Webster's dictionary defines it as "long and patient endurance of offense" (*Webster's Ninth New Collegiate Dictionary*). I don't like suffering even a little!

TV sitcoms often model impatience in family life. Angry flare-ups are staged to seem humorous. Idiosyncrasies are shown as justifiable reason for unkind rhetoric and unchristian reactions. Generation gaps are exaggerated. Clever scriptwriters write a comeback or barb for every situation, and they can resolve any problem in thirty minutes minus time for commercials. The virtues of patience and long-suffering are seldom if ever portrayed. In Christ-centered homes, irritations, conflicts, miscommunications, and competition still exist, but unlike families portrayed on television, the gospel gives examples of people who may raise an eyebrow but not the roof. President Thomas S. Monson said, "There seems to be an unending supply of trouble for one and all. Our problem is that we often expect instantaneous solutions, forgetting that frequently the heavenly virtue of patience is required" ("Look to God and Live," *Ensign,* May 1998, 52). The family setting is the ideal laboratory in which to practice, exercise, develop, and learn patience.

Have you noticed that your children act with more patience or impatience right after you do? Both patience and impatience are contagious. Patience is sometimes measured in minutes; at other times patience is enduring situations that might never get better. Patience is the power to stay focused. Patience is the ability not to complain or, in Book of Mormon language, murmur. Patience is persisting with a calm serenity that smoothes over the rough places, the routine bumps and jolts in the road of life. Paul describes how "tribulation worketh patience; And patience, experience; and experience, hope" (Rom. 5:3–4).

Impatience, on the other hand, shows annoyance. Little irritations become mountains and mountains become volcanic. Impatience is edginess. An impatient person is hard to live with. An impatient person seems to be just one sentence away from an argument. An impatient person looks for offenses. Impatience acts and then thinks. On the other hand, patience thinks and then acts. Patience is needed in every relationship—with children, husbands, employers, friends, and especially with the Lord's timing.

I heard a talk many years ago when I was just beginning my mothering. The speaker said that home life would be smoother and happier if the mother left three things unsaid daily. I've tried it, and it is a good exercise in patience. Don't add that snide comment or always have to have the last word or even try to be the center of conversations. Resist the temptation to say any of the phrases that translate into "I told you so." Don't add your zesty bit of information when discussion turns to backbiting or gossip. The amazing thing to me about not saying something negative or snide is that at the moment of temptation, saying that thing seems like the most important thing in the world. But when I've been able to practice patience and not say whatever it was that I thought was so crucial, I have noticed that within a few hours I can't even remember what it was that I was going to say.

One woman told of her experience of leaving three things unsaid. She said at first she thought the idea had nothing to do with patience, but the Spirit encouraged her to leave three things unsaid for a week as a trial. She reported it was one of the hardest things she had ever done. She could hardly stop herself from having the last word or being snippy when she felt offended. It was almost impossible to keep silent when she could have made her point with a clever barb. But she kept working at it. She actually kept track to see if three unsaid words or phrases could in fact make a difference. Often at bedtime she would still have a couple of things to leave unsaid. She said that she noticed that over the process of several months, her family life became more pleasant. It's been ten years since she made her first goal to leave three things unsaid, and a remarkable change has evolved. Although at first she struggled and had to figuratively tape her mouth shut, now, a decade later, her patience is remarkable. The love between her husband and her shows in their every conversation. Whereas it used to take a week for them to get over an argument, misunderstandings are now resolved in minutes. And another very significant change has occurred. Right after she stopped saying hurtful things, it seems that her husband and children began speaking more kindly too. This mother reports that an inner change of heart also resulted. Not only does she not *say* those things anymore, but rarely does she even *think* them! (And can you believe there is another astonishing benefit from leaving three things unsaid—you learn more. How? Because when you aren't talking you are listening!)

Patience in enduring difficult situations often has a positive result. A couple in our ward went on a mission to England and met a woman who had joined the Church twenty years ago. Her children had joined, but her husband had not. *Supportive* would not be a word to describe him. He had tried various tactics to discourage her Church membership and activity. Recently, as I was walking into our meetinghouse, this missionary couple, who have been home less than a year, introduced me to a couple visiting them from England. Later, in sacrament meeting, the bishop invited the husband to bear his testimony. He told of his wife's baptism, about his efforts to separate her from her newly found church, and about the couple from our ward who came into their home and showed him the gospel in action. He was baptized nine months ago. His wife had been patient twenty-one years and ten months! Patience is staying power. Patience is enduring. Sometimes patience works miracles.

QUESTIONS AND ANSWERS

How important a question is depends, of course, on what the answer is. "How are you?" is usually no more than a casual greeting, but it takes on serious overtones when asked by a paramedic at an accident scene. A fifteen-year-old boy asking on fast day, "When will dinner be ready?" is much different than the same question from a husband who'd like to finish a project before dinner. Assessing the person, setting, and situation and trying to understand both sides of the question-and-answer process are always important. This assessment can become absolutely crucial when eternal questions are asked, such as when a missionary asks, "Will you be baptized?" and the bishop asks, "Are you worthy to enter the temple?" If the importance of a question is judged by its answer, fourteen-year-old Joseph Smith's question is one of the greatest: "My object in going to inquire of the Lord was to know which of all the sects was right, that I might know which to join" (JS—H 1:18).

In church, questions are sung: "Did you think to pray?" and "Where can I turn for peace?" And the scriptures are full of questions. In Alma 5, for example, there are forty-one question marks!

Questions have blessed the earth with revealed truths. How did the Word of Wisdom come to be? Because Joseph Smith was prompted to ponder the issue and inquired of the Lord. How did the instructions come concerning the correct mode of baptism? Because Joseph Smith and Oliver Cowdery asked for knowledge concerning the procedure. Why is there a Primary organization today? Because Aurelia Spencer Rogers asked Eliza R. Snow, general Relief Society president asked, "Could there not be an organization for little boys, and have them trained to make better men?" (*Encyclopedia of Mormonism*, 3:1146). Sister Snow asked President John Taylor the same question, and the result was the Primary organization.

The Savior told the story of the good Samaritan because a young lawyer asked, "And who is my neighbor?" (see Luke 10:29). Doctrine and Covenants 121 came because of Joseph Smith's pleading question "Oh, God, where art thou?" (v. 1). Why do we have recorded in John 13–15 such detail about the conversation during the Last Supper? Because five of the Apostles asked questions. Without two other questions from those early Apostles in Christ's time, we may not have the knowledge found in Matthew 24: "Tell us, when shall these things be?" and "What shall be the sign of thy coming and of the end of world?" (v. 3).

But what does all this have to do with you? What a good question! Glad you asked! When someone asks a question, you get clues as to what is going on in the questioner's brain. Listening to questions helps you get a pulse on others' lives. Another reason questions are so important is that the way questions are answered sets the tone of the home and determines future communication success or failure between husband and wife, parents and children (especially teens), and siblings. When a question is asked, if I respond with, "Can't you see how busy I am?" or, "You asked me that yesterday," I don't show respect or love or patience, and I can be absolutely sure that I will get those same responses back in a few hours or years. The way I respond to family members' questions and the questions I ask them show how much I value them.

If your life is like mine, 90 percent of the questions children ask are routine—the time or place of this and that, permission to go or do, wanting something, needing something, or housekeeping questions—"Where are my blue pants?" and "Do I really have to clean my room before I go?" And there's always the question that begins at age three, "Why?" which never seems to go away and never has a satisfying answer. I have found that even the way I answer mundane questions is important. The first problem for me is hearing the question. Does the child always have to repeat their question because I am too busy with my own thoughts and concerns? I've discovered that mundane questions may mask unspoken concerns: "Am I important to you?" "Do you really care about me?" By making more mistakes than I'd like to admit, I've learned a few techniques:

- Listen to the question.

- Give eye contact.

- Smile and/or touch the child when appropriate.

- Stop what you are doing.

- Acknowledge the question. It may be with an answer, a question in return, or "I don't know. Let me think about it for a minute."

- Answer softly, respectfully, and as simply as possible.

- Admit that you don't know, if you don't.

- Ask follow-up questions if appropriate. Even probing questions may be in order in some settings and situations. Questions may include: Where are you going? What time will you be home? With whom are you going? How can I help? Are you feeling hurt (or sick or angry or sad)? How do you feel about that? How much does it cost? Is there more to the story? Why were you late? What did you learn today? Will you help me? Where did you get it? Whose is it? Did you say you are sorry? How will you make it right? Do you know how much I love you?

Things I try never to do:

- Discourage questions.

- Discourage the person who asks the question.

- Think the question is the question. (Oftentimes the question masks a need, an insecurity, a dilemma, a hope.)

- Let my face or voice betray negative feelings. (I've been told more than once by more than one child that I suffer from the "freak-out syndrome," which is overreacting. Another name for this response pattern is "newspaper-headline-itis." One little hint that something may be wrong, and I lose all sense of proportion. My brain skips over wisdom and past experience, and I react and see what's happening as tomorrow's shocking newspaper headline, rather than calmly working through the situation to get to the facts.)

Studying the examples of the Apostles and Joseph Smith asking questions, it occurred to me that when I lack knowledge, I can ask Him who knows all the questions and all the answers. He can even help me know what I should pray for and for whom I should pray. Is there a spiritual gift I should be cultivating? How can I make better use of . . . ? How can I be a better wife (mother, daughter, sister, friend, follower of His Son)? How can I be the answer to another's prayer? His answers will come as I humbly admit that I know far too few answers. I feel most blessed when His answers come as a beloved hymn describes: "He answers privately, reaches my reaching" ("Where Can I Turn for Peace?" *Hymns*, 129).

Questions and answers are so much a part of good mothering—so much a part of being a good daughter of God.

COMING TO THE WELL THIRSTY

On the wall behind my computer hangs a poster I made. It has a picture and five words on it. The picture is the Samaritan woman at the well from the gospel art series. You've probably seen it. Jesus is sitting; she is standing. Her hands rest on her empty vessel as she listens to the Savior. The five words are "Come to the well thirsty."

> Jesus . . . sat thus on the well . . . [when] there cometh a woman of Samaria to draw water: Jesus saith unto her, Give me to drink. . . .Then saith the woman of Samaria unto him, How is it that thou, being a Jew, askest drink of me, which am a woman of Samaria? for the Jews have no dealings with the Samaritans. Jesus answered and said unto her, If thou knewest the gift of God, and who it is that saith to thee, Give me to drink; thou wouldest have asked of him, and he would have given thee living water. The woman saith unto him, Sir, thou hast nothing to draw with, and the well is deep: from whence then hast thou that living water? Art thou greater than our father Jacob, which gave us the well, and drank thereof himself, and his children, and his cattle? Jesus answered and said unto her, Whosoever drinketh of this water shall thirst again: But whosoever drinketh of the water that I shall give him shall never thirst; but the water that I shall give him shall be in him a well of water springing up into everlasting life. The woman saith unto him, Sir, give me this water, that I thirst not, neither come hither to draw. Jesus saith unto her, Go,

call thy husband, and come hither. The woman answered
and said, I have no husband. Jesus said unto her, Thou hast
well said, I have no husband: For thou hast had five
husbands; and he whom thou now hast is not thy husband:
in that saidst thou truly. The woman saith unto him, Sir, I
perceive that thou art a prophet. . . . I know that Messias
cometh, which is called Christ: when he is come, he will
tell us all things. Jesus saith unto her, I that speak unto
thee am he. . . . The woman then left her waterpot, and
went her way into the city, and saith to the men, Come,
see a man, which told me all things that ever I did: is not
this the Christ? Then they went out of the city, and came
unto him. (John 4:6–30)

One day while I was reading this account, it occurred to me that I
was the woman at the well, and I wondered, do I come thirsty? Do I
come to the well with an empty vessel? Do I recognize the Savior?
"Whosoever drinketh of this water [regular H_2O] shall thirst again:
But whosoever drinketh of the water that I shall give him . . . shall be
in him a well of water springing up into everlasting life."

What lessons can I learn from the woman of Samaria on how to
come to the well thirsty?

She arrived at the well at exactly the right moment. Was it a
chance meeting? The Savior gave other examples of meetings such as
this that were no coincidence: "But I tell you of a truth, many widows
were in Israel in the days of Elias, when the heaven was shut up three
years and six months, when great famine was throughout all the land;
But unto none of them was Elias [Elijah] sent, save unto Sarepta
[Zerephath], a city of Sidon, unto a woman that was a widow" (Luke
4:25–26). Or this example: "And many lepers were in Israel in the
time of Eliseus the prophet; and none of them was cleansed, saving
Naaman the Syrian" (Luke 4:27).

Jesus gave these examples of the widow of Zarephath and Naaman to
make the point to the people of Nazareth that it was not by chance that
He was there at that moment in their synagogue reading to them Isaiah's
words about what the Messiah would do. He was there to declare His
divinity: "This day is this scripture fulfilled in your ears" (Luke 4:21).

So we may assume that meetings such as these are not happenstance. Jesus was waiting at the well for her, but how did the woman get to the well at the right time? We can only believe that she followed promptings. In John 4, I found eleven lessons I can learn from this Samaritan woman.

Lesson 1: Unknowingly, she followed promptings to insure she was at the right place at the right time.

Lesson 2: She was willing to be taught. She listened and asked questions: Why would you ask me for a drink? How do you plan to get the water, for you have nothing to draw with and the well is deep?

Lesson 3: She showed deference as she addressed the Savior with respect. "Sir . . ."

Lesson 4: She began to put the pieces together as to what she was learning and with whom she was speaking, as evidenced by another question: "Are you greater than Jacob whose well this is?"

Lesson 5: She openly acknowledged her feelings: "Sir, I perceive that thou art a prophet" (v. 19).

Lesson 6: She asked for a drink of living water; perceiving that He was greater than Jacob and feeling a desire to partake of the living water, she said: "Give me this water" (v. 15).

Lesson 7: The Savior gave her an additional witness by revealing that He knew about her personal life. She then shared her understanding and evidenced her faith: "The woman saith unto him, I know that Messias cometh, which is called Christ: when he is come, he will tell us all things" (v. 25).

Lesson 8: When she acknowledged His omniscience, He revealed Himself to her: "Jesus saith unto her, I that speak unto thee am he" (v. 26).

Lesson 9: She acted on her knowledge. She was so excited about what she had learned and from whom she had learned it that she left her waterpot and went joyfully to spread the news (vv. 28–29).

Lesson 10: She bore testimony: "Come, see a man, which told me all things that ever I did: is not this the Christ?" (v. 29).

Lesson 11: She brought others to meet the Savior: "Then they went out of the city, and came unto him" (v. 30).

Sharing testimony is the desire of witnesses of Jesus Christ. Once converted, they spread the good news of His gospel. The shepherds who were "keeping watch over their flocks by night" (Luke 2:8) are examples of this. (Again, likely it's no coincidence that those specific shepherds were watching those specific sheep when the angel told them of the Savior's birth.) What did they do when the angels had gone away? They "came with haste" (v. 16), "made [it] known abroad" (v. 17), and "returned, glorifying and praising God" (v. 20).

The Samaritan woman went with haste, even forgetting to get the water she had come for, made it known abroad, and returned with others glorifying and praising God (John 4:28–30). I hope I come to the well—the scriptures, the temple, sacrament meeting, Relief Society, Sunday School, stake conference, general conference—thirsty. From past experience I know that living water tastes delicious. "Blessed are they which do . . . thirst after righteousness: for they shall be filled" (Matt. 5:6).

UNANSWERED PRAYER?

Garth Brooks sings, "Thank God for unanswered prayers." As a high school student, his song goes, he prayed often and intensely that his girlfriend would become his wife. He promised God that if he could marry her, he'd never ask for another thing for the rest of his life. It didn't happen. Years later, the character in the song saw this high school sweetheart at an event, looked at his own wife, and thanked God for not granting his youthful petitions. He sings, "Some of God's greatest gifts are unanswered prayers" (planetgarth.com/lyrics/). The question is: Did his prayers really go unanswered?

Prayer is the most efficient communication possible. Any person can think or say words that are immediately transferred to our Heavenly Father. On the topic of prayer, the Bible Dictionary states:

> As soon as we learn the true relationship in which we stand toward God (namely, God is our Father, and we are his children), then at once prayer becomes natural and instinctive on our part (Matt. 7:7–11). Many of the so-called difficulties about prayer arise from forgetting this relationship. Prayer is the act by which the will of the Father and the will of the child are brought into correspondence with each other. The object of prayer is not to change the will of God, but to secure for ourselves and for others blessings that God is already willing to grant, but that are made conditional on our asking for them. Blessings require some work or effort on our part before we can obtain them. Prayer is a form of work, and is an

appointed means for obtaining the highest of all blessings. (753)

A mother can develop a special link to the heavens, with the help of the Holy Ghost, as she calls upon her Father to help her parent His children. There are times, however, that most every mother feels her pleadings are being lodged in the insulation in the roof. But if a sparrow doesn't fall without the Lord's notice, can any righteous prayer go unanswered? In Garth Brooks's case the answer was, "Garth, this isn't the girl for you. Be patient."

Why are some prayers answered immediately and others seemingly not at all? Quickly answered prayers may produce testimonies that prayer works. You might interpret quickly answered prayers as earnest money, showing that Heavenly Father is attentive and aware of your needs and that more answers are forthcoming. Prayers that take longer to get answered show that there is a plan for each person and that God's timing is His alone. Some answers are simply "No." When a child asks her mother for a dollar, whether it's a yes or no that follows, it's still an answer. The fact is, "No" is an answer. "No" answers may cause mortals to ask, "Why?"

President Kimball answered:

> If all the sick for whom we pray were healed, if all the righteous were protected and the wicked destroyed, the whole program of the Father would be annulled and the basic principle of the gospel, agency, would be ended. No man would have to live by faith.

> Should all prayers be immediately answered according to our selfish desires and our limited understanding, then there would be little or no suffering, sorrow, disappointment, or even death, and if these were not, there would also be no joy, success, resurrection, nor eternal life and godhood.

> Being human, we would expel from our lives physical pain and mental anguish and assure ourselves of continual ease

and comfort, but if we were to close the doors upon sorrow and distress, we might be excluding our greatest friends and benefactors. Suffering can make saints of people as they learn patience, long-suffering, and self-mastery. (*Faith Precedes the Miracle*, 97–98)

Hebrews 5:8 states that even though Jesus was the Son of God, He, too, learned by the things which He suffered. Two things are certain about prayer: first, God hears, and second, God answers.

Understanding that "prayer is not to change the will of God," but to bring His will and our will into correspondence with each other, brings another issue forward. Is there a way to have fewer "no" or seemingly unanswered prayers? Yes, there is. If I realize that "prayer is a form of work," if I take thought before praying and ask the Spirit to guide me in knowing for what things I should pray, if I study issues out in my mind, if I ask for the ability to see the big picture, I will have more successful experiences in asking according to Heavenly Father's will.

James and Nephi teach another principle about prayer. "Ye ask, and receive not, because ye ask amiss, that ye may consume it upon your lusts" (James 4:3). "Yea, I know that God will give liberally to him that asketh. Yea, my God will give me, if I ask not amiss" (2 Ne. 4:35).

When the adversity wolf has paid me a visit, my days, and too often my nights, are filled with continual prayer. In those bleak hours when I've asked for the Spirit to guide my prayers, my prayers become more specific and fervent and stretch beyond the insulation in the roof. On one of the precious occasions when I faithfully reached for Him, I wrote:

> *His arms outstretch; He quiets fear;*
> *He whispers peace; His message clear.*
> *The veil thins; His presence felt*
> *And all because I paused and knelt.*

God, our Heavenly Father, is aware of you and me. He reveals Himself in the way He answers the prayers of His children—sometimes immediately and sometimes in His own omniscient way for His own eternal purposes. But one thing is guaranteed: there is no such thing as an unanswered prayer.

THE CURE FOR THE
DIVORCE EPIDEMIC

As a Gospel Doctrine teacher I learned the Old Testament by teaching it. Week after week I marveled as the Old Testament unfolded before me. In my mind the written words became digital-quality color and sound as the patriarchs and prophets became real. The week I was to teach the events in Numbers 21, the plague of the fiery serpents, I prayed to find a latter-day equivalent. In my mind I could see Moses, the latter-day prophet of that time, holding up the brazen (brass) serpent. The story goes like this:

Flying, fiery serpents descended on the children of Israel, causing "much people of Israel" to die from the serpents' lethal bite. In fear for their lives, "the people came to Moses, and said . . . pray unto the Lord, that he take away the serpents from us. And Moses prayed for the people. And the Lord said unto Moses, Make thee a fiery serpent, and set it upon a pole: and it shall come to pass, that every one that is bitten, when he looketh upon it, shall live. And Moses made a serpent of brass, and put it upon a pole, and it came to pass, that if a serpent had bitten any man, when he beheld the serpent of brass, he lived" (Num. 21:6–9).

It was that simple. The prophet made a serpent out of brass and affixed it to a pole. The children of Israel had only to look at it and they would be healed. Therefore everyone looked and was healed, right?

No! Nephi comments on the sad ending to the story. He says that many did not look "because of the simpleness of the way, or the easiness of it" (1 Ne. 17:41). Why? Why would those suffering not look and be healed? Were they stubborn, rebellious, faithless? How could they choose death with such a simple alternative available? What is the excuse to die rather than take advantage of an uncomplicated, sure cure?

As I contemplated the tragedy of the story, a modern-day equivalent did come to my mind. There is a lethal plague, a fatal disease in our time. This deadly serpent bites over half of the people who get married, and this serpent's bite is much worse than the serpent's sting of Moses' time. Today's serpent causes the death of covenants, and the subsequent pain affects not only the person bitten but also the person's spouse, children, parents, siblings, extended family, friends and neighbors. Members of the Church cry out to our prophet, begging him to pray to the Lord for a remedy.

Just as looking up at the brass serpent on the pole healed people of Moses' time, so can people be healed from today's plague—divorce—by looking upon something President Hinckley has given us. That something is "The Family: A Proclamation to the World," which states principles that can restore troubled marriages and families to health.

"The Family: A Proclamation to the World" is the word of the Lord to us through the First Presidency and the Quorum of the Twelve Apostles. In its nine paragraphs, the Lord's healing power is given in simple, easy language. Our prophet holds it up for us to look upon. We get copies of the proclamation, frame them, and hang them on the walls of our homes, but do we look at the words with faith to mend troubled relationships? It seems that "because of the simpleness of the way, or the easiness of it," the proclamation is considered to be of little consequence other than being a nice addition to the decor of our homes.

Why don't we who are bitten—those of us who are experiencing a sick marriage—at least try the proclamation? Are we stubborn, rebellious, faithless? Does the proclamation seem too simple or too easy? Do we think the cures of the world will work better?

The parallel is there. The brazen serpent beckoned; "The Family: A Proclamation to the World" beckons. The Lord spoke through Moses; the Lord spoke through President Hinckley.

The proclamation is simple. For example, in its seventh paragraph, nine righteous principles for successful marriages and families are listed: faith, prayer, repentance, forgiveness, respect, love, compassion, work, and wholesome recreational activities. Read it. Study it. Obey it. The proclamation is a brass serpent for our time. Look and be healed.

MISBEHAVIOR

When your child is misbehaving, do you take a few seconds to analyze why? If you do, it can be both bad and good. It's bad because mothers often make excuses for the child. "Oh, he's just tired," when spunking is a better definition, or "She's just trying to give the baby a hug," when *strangling* is a better word. You can't always correctly judge a child's motives by his actions, and even if you could, making excuses for him is never a good idea. Mothers, especially first-time mothers, make excuses for their child's bad behavior, which sets up potentially troublesome patterns for the future. When the child hears his mother making excuses for his behavior over and over, the child realizes that he isn't required to take responsibility for his actions. He subconsciously thinks, "Hey, this is a good deal. Whenever I misbehave, Mom quickly steps in to justify my actions." If you have the tendency to excuse your child's bad behavior, catch yourself doing it and stop.

The good part of analyzing why a child is misbehaving is that you can better deal with the situation in positive, helpful ways. When your child misbehaves, take a second before responding to decide if one of the three most common factors of misbehavior—hunger, fatigue, or boredom—is the cause. If it is, don't make an excuse; take action. A bored child is often a misbehaving child. (With my children and now with my grandchildren, my rule is that if the child or grandchild says, "I'm bored," it means the child doesn't have enough to do, and a job is found for him or her. As you can imagine, no one says, "I'm bored" when I'm within hearing range.) And every mother knows how she feels when she is tired or hungry or both. The world always looks better after a good night's rest and with a full stomach. These three intrinsic factors are the simplest to identify and the easiest to rectify.

Another common cause of misbehavior is the need for more adult attention. Do the child's actions say, "Pay attention to me" or, "I need you"? Children will do whatever it takes to get the adult attention they need—usually without realizing it—to feel important and loved. Mothers need to know how crucial their awareness and focus are to a child. Wise mothers know that children will do almost anything to get their mother's attention. If positive, acceptable ways don't work, then not-so-acceptable ways will be tried. Negative attention, even punishment, is still attention to an attention-needy child. One of the truest of all mothering principles is that behavior that gets noticed gets repeated. That is so important it deserves repetition. *Behavior that gets noticed gets repeated.* So if a child misbehaves to get attention and the mother gives that attention, the attention ratifies the behavior (teaches the child that he or she has been successful) and the behavior will be repeated. Since children differ in how much attention they need, mothers must pray for guidance in finding the balance between either smothering the child with too much attention and thereby creating an emotionally dependent child, or creating a deficiency in which the child feels emotionally abandoned because of lack of attention.

The next category of reasons for a child's misbehavior includes the bad things that happen to him because of the sins of adults in his life—unhappy marriage, separation or divorce, parental dysfunction, criminal activity, addiction, or abuse (whether it is substance, emotional, physical, psychological, or verbal). These factors compound a child's view of the world to an extent that is hard to overstate. However, children who experience sad events in life—injury, illness, accident, financial hardship, or death of a loved one—are usually not scarred in the same negative ways as those children affected by sin. But whatever bad or sad things happen in a child's life, where love, faith, and fortitude are the family's tools for responding, the child copes better because he feels more secure.

One national tutoring company teaches a good method to preclude misbehavior. It expects good behavior, and it rewards good behavior. During any given hour of instruction, a teacher will give a student between zero and twenty tokens for effort, not necessarily performance. If a child misbehaves, threatening to take tokens back quickly gets the child on task again. The tokens purchase items from the incentive store—games, toys, and gift certificates. The results are predictable. Children respond to the constructive, the optimistic. Mothers who are warm and affectionate, who are positive and supportive, who remember that praise raises, who know they are their child's mirror reflecting how the child is valued; mothers who listen, listen, listen, who give the child choices and involve the child in decision making in age-appropriate ways; and mothers who set limits, stay firm, and are boringly consistent create an environment in which children thrive. There was a catch phrase a few years back that deserves to be recycled: "Catch your child being good." Acknowledging the good helps diminish bad behavior.

Be proactive, not retroactive. Prevention always beats repair. Not making excuses for your child, analyzing the child's behavior so that you will respond appropriately, and using preventative techniques, such as catching your child being good or using a reward system, will help you sidestep many episodes of misbehavior.

WRITE AND SPEAK
FOR POSTERITY

Do you have a letter from your grandfather, mother, teacher, or friend that you have saved, read, and reread over the years, a letter you cherish? Maria Jefferson received such a letter from her father, Thomas.

To Maria Jefferson, New York, April 11, 1790:

> *Where are you, my dear Maria? How do you do? How are you occupied? Write me a letter by the first post, and answer me all these questions. Tell me whether you see the sun rise every day? How many pages a day you read in Don Quixote? How far you are advanced in him? Whether you repeat a grammar lesson every day? What else you read? How many hours a day you sew? Whether you have an opportunity of continuing your music? Whether you know how to make a pudding yet, to cut out a beefsteak, to sow spinach, or to set a hen? Be good, my dear, as I have always found you; ever everybody's faults be forgotten, as you would wish yours to be; take more pleasure in giving what is best to another than in having it yourself and then all the world will love you, and I more than all the world. If your sister is with you, kiss her and tell her how much I love her also, and present my affections to Mr. Randolph. Love your aunt and uncle and be dutiful and obliging to them for all their kindness to you. What would you do without them and with such a vagrant for father? Say to both of them a thousand affectionate things for me; and adieu, my dear Maria. Thomas Jefferson* (Edwin Morris Betts and James Adam Bear, comp., *The Family Letters of Thomas Jefferson*, 52).

Have you written such a letter for someone to cherish? With the tremendous popularity of scrapbooking, many fortunate children have a mother who photographs them at every step of their lives. These mothers collect and arrange the pictures in artistic volumes, which is all good. The old axiom, "A picture is worth a thousand words," is currently in vogue. However, an artistic scrapbook with a thousand photos and only few names, dates, and places cheats the child of the personal, intimate blessing of his mother's descriptions and feelings. Oh, how blessed is the child who has both photos and words!

In Thomas Jefferson's letter to Maria, his character opens up to us. Even though it was written more than two hundred years ago, we know of his love and his expectations for Maria. We know not only what is important to him but also how important she is to him. We identify with his longing to be with her. We see that he is not only expressing love and concern, but also teaching her. How valuable are his words!

Write to and about your children. Record their cute ways during childhood and their progress and growth on the way to adulthood. Use special occasions such as birth, baptism, and graduation for expressions of love and confidence from you—the sister, daughter, granddaughter, mother, aunt, grandmother, great-grandmother, or friend—in writing.

Those who record history, in a sense, make history. One such example is Wilford Woodruff, who helped record the history of the Church:

> Although Wilford Woodruff (1833–1898) served as Church historian from 1883 to 1889, he made his greatest contributions to Church history as assistant Church historian from 1856 to 1883. He was the prime motivator behind a project to publish a biography of each man who had served in the Quorum of the Twelve Apostles, and was instrumental in preparing the sermons of Joseph Smith for publication in the *History of the Church*. Woodruff's journals, which he kept with diligence from the time he joined the Church until a few weeks before his death, proved

invaluable in compiling the histories of Joseph Smith and Brigham Young. (*Encyclopedia of Mormonism,* 4:590)

Wilford Woodruff was also the first prophet to record his voice for posterity. It was recorded on a wax cylinder. In less than four hundred words, he bears witness, as an eyewitness, that "Joseph Smith was a true prophet of God, ordained of God to lay the foundation of His Church and kingdom in the last dispensation and fulness of times." He tells of an experience when the Prophet was teaching the Twelve. "His face was as clear as amber, and he was covered with a power that I have never seen in any man in the flesh before. . . . In all his testimonies to us the power of God was visibly manifest in [him]." President Woodruff bears testimony of his first-hand knowledge of temple endowments. "I received my own endowments under his hands and direction, and I know they are true principles." His last words on the cylinder: "This is my testimony, spoken by myself into a talking machine on this the nineteenth day of March 1897, in the ninety-first year of my age" ("Record Transcription," *New Era,* Jan. 1972, 66).

My walking partner of more than a decade had, and I suppose still has, an extraordinarily beautiful singing voice. Three years ago when she was diagnosed with leukemia, she began a serious effort to write her personal history, histories of her children, and to make recordings of herself singing with her husband, children, and grandchildren. She completed the histories she wanted to write and made many recordings. She left behind as much of herself as possible. Your words are as valuable to your family as hers are to her family. Record your voice on tape. If you play an instrument or sing, record that too!

Those people who keep records are the ones who in reality make history. Think what is remembered because of Moses, Nephi, Mormon, Joseph Smith, and Wilford Woodruff. Think how our cumulative national memory has been preserved through men who wrote—Thomas Jefferson, James Madison, Abraham Lincoln.

If you want your life to be remembered, write about it in a journal or history. Include not only the important, but also the mundane, so that someone in the future who reads it will have an idea of what your day-to-day life was like. Include talks you've given, your thoughts, aspirations, testimony, and commentary on events in your life and in the world. And do it while the memories and emotions are fresh. The historian makes history. What is recorded is ultimately all that is remembered and known. Extend your influence. Write and speak to posterity!

ZION:
THE BEST OF TIMES

As a docent in the Museum of Church History and Art, I am asked about the word *Zion* often because it figures prominently in the Kirtland and Nauvoo periods of the Church. I've had to study and prepare some ready answers. The basic definition of Zion is "the pure in heart," but Zion is also a place where the pure in heart live. (So Zion can be a person or a place.) Zion is the name of the righteous city built by Enoch that was taken to heaven. (Moses 7:19 tells that the complete name of Enoch's city was "the City of Holiness, even Zion.") The scripture I like best on the subject states, "The Lord called his people Zion, because they were of one heart and one mind, and dwelt in righteousness; and there was no poor among them" (Moses 7:18). The prophecies are clear that in the latter days a Zion city will be built near Jackson County, Missouri.

I tell museum visitors that Zion can be wherever they are if they are pure in heart. Which brings up the next question: "What does it mean to be pure in heart?" I looked up *pure*. It means "free from sin or guilt; blameless. A person becomes pure when his thoughts and actions are clean in every way. A person who has committed sin can become pure through faith in Jesus Christ, repentance, and receiving the ordinances of the gospel" (Guide to the Scriptures, lds.org). The scripture that helps here is Psalm 24:4–5: "He that hath clean hands, and a pure heart . . . shall receive the blessings from the Lord."

The tenth article of faith also teaches about Zion. "We believe in the literal gathering of Israel and in the restoration of the Ten Tribes; that Zion (the New Jerusalem) will be built upon the American continent; that Christ will reign personally upon the earth; and, that the earth will be renewed and receive its paradisiacal glory." It isn't often, but once in a while I get to this point with a visitor in the museum. When they hear that "Christ will reign personally upon the earth," most of them express incredulity but also hope that such a glorious time is possible, wondering what it will be like.

Since there is so little detail about Enoch and his city of Zion, the only example of what a Zion society might be like is found in 4 Nephi. The record states that the disciples of Jesus formed a church of Christ in all the land and that they baptized and conferred the gift of the Holy Ghost on all who repented. And all the people repented and were converted. There were no contentions or disputes. Every person dealt justly with every other person. There were no rich or poor because they had all things in common. The disciples of Jesus exercised their priesthood and healed the sick, raised the dead, cured the lame, blind, and deaf, and worked mighty miracles. And the people prospered and multiplied and became a delightsome people. They kept the commandments they had personally received from the Lord. They fasted and prayed and met together often to hear the word of the Lord. The people all had the love of God in their hearts.

> And there were no envyings, nor strifes, nor tumults, nor whoredoms, nor lyings, nor murders, nor any manner of lasciviousness; and surely there could not be a happier people among all the people who had been created by the hand of God. There were no robbers, nor murderers, neither were there Lamanites, nor any manner of -ites; but they were in one, the children of Christ, and heirs to the kingdom of God. And how blessed were they! For the Lord did bless them in all their doings; yea, even they were blessed and prospered until an hundred and ten years had passed away; and the first generation from Christ had passed away, and there was no contention in all the land. (4 Ne. 1:16–18)

As you well know, after about two hundred years, evil devices slowly began to infiltrate. In two hundred more years, a war of extinction took place and the Nephite nation was annihilated.

Comparing the Nephite civilization to the Zion to be built in Jackson County, Missouri, is limited because three conditions will be different: Jesus Christ will reign personally; Satan will be bound by the righteousness of the people; and it will last for one thousand years. Oh! How I look forward to being a citizen of the New Jerusalem! I can think of nothing better. It will be the very best of all times to live on the earth.

But while I am waiting for a Zion society, I should concentrate on making this time and circumstance in which I live the best of times. Because of the influence of one of my sons-in-law, Terry, I have thought about the "best of times." Terry likes to make family movies, and because of his computer editing skills, his work is quite professional. The name of his family's video is "The Best of Times," and he uses the STYX song of the 1980s, "The Best of Times," as the theme song. The video shows Terry and Michelle's family doing very normal everyday things—Christmases and birthdays, new babies in mother's arms, learning to ride a tricycle, taking karate, singing, playing the piano, playing games, running on the beach, being with extended family. It's all there, just an ordinary family living life. At the end, the theme song comes, and the words "These are the best of times" appear on the screen again and again as a moment in time is captured showing each individual family member. The song continues, "Our memories of yesterday . . . some rain . . . some shine. . . . We'll take the best . . . forget the rest . . . and someday we'll find . . . these are the best of times." Then there is a collage of family scenes and more music; and the words appear again on the screen, and a few more family scenes, and then the words "Actually, it's barely the beginning."

What does Terry mean, "Actually, it's barely the beginning"? Is this barely the beginning of the good times? Is their ordinary life the best life gets? Is the load of burdens they carry going to go away? I think that the words "Actually, it's only the beginning" mean that no matter what happens, these are the best of times because there is nothing else. Terry will take the rain and the shine, forget the rest, and someday he'll find that these *are* the best of times. Whatever is going on today can be the best of times if I trust in God's plan. The good times in this life are only the beginning with an eternal family; there are a thousand years of Zion and an eternity after that.

Remember the best of times of the past, and look forward to the even better times to come. For the Lord said, "I, the Lord, am merciful and gracious unto those who fear me, and delight to honor those who serve me in righteousness and in truth unto the end. Great shall be their reward and eternal shall be their glory. And to them will I reveal all mysteries, yea, all the hidden mysteries of my kingdom from days of old, and for ages to come, will I make known unto them the good pleasure of my will concerning all things pertaining to my kingdom. Yea, even the wonders of eternity shall they know, and things to come will I show them, even the things of many generations. And their wisdom shall be great, and their understanding reach to heaven; and before them the wisdom of the wise shall perish, and the understanding of the prudent shall come to naught. For by my Spirit will I enlighten them, and by my power will I make known unto them the secrets of my will—yea, even those things which eye has not seen, nor ear heard, nor yet entered into the heart of man" (D&C 76:5–10). Zion and whatever comes after is certainly something worth anticipating.

RESPECT:
HOW TO TEACH IT

Respect could be defined as admiration, deference, reverence, or esteem. Disrespect is contempt, disregard, or impertinence. When is the best time to teach your child respect?

Mothers teach respect or disrespect from the beginning. Contemplate the future for an infant whose 2:00 A.M. crying is met by a mother who nurses him while stroking his face and telling him how beautiful he is, versus that of one who is met in the wee hours by an angry, exhausted mother who nurses him while chiding him for not sleeping through the night and by telling him to hurry up so that she can get some sleep. When is the best time to teach a child about respect? The answer is right now, today, and every day.

When comparing example and didactic teaching, example teaches as with a megaphone. "What you are speaks so loudly I can't hear what you say" is an oft-quoted saying that reminds me how powerful my example is. If I, though distressed, say supportive words about the police officer who just gave me a ticket, I teach respect for law. When I pray vocally for the President of the Church and the president of the United States, I teach respect for authority. When I tell a store clerk that she rang up the purchase incorrectly and I owe more money, I teach respect for others' money and for the commandments. When my children see me rubbing my husband's back and thanking him for being a good provider, I teach respect for the marriage covenant. When I give time and loving service to my aging mother-in-law, I teach respect for family and the elderly.

I have made the mistake of thinking children will know innately how to be respectful, that example is enough. As essential as example is, I still need to instruct—to be proactive—to teach the values and attitudes I want my children to develop. In an informal setting, I can teach a more respectful way to handle a situation. Family home evening is a good time for more formal instruction. Children love to role-play, and even teens will usually participate. Consider playing a game; "Let's pretend that . . ." or role-play and practice acting respectful and showing respect in a variety of simulated situations. For example, you can ask your children what they would do if:

- Your elderly neighbor forgets to bring in his garbage can.

- You answer the phone and can't quite understand who the speaker is because of his accent.

- You and a mother pushing a stroller are heading toward the mall entrance at the same time.

- You are having a party but don't know if you should invite a boy who is in a wheelchair.

- You are in a hurry, but your little brother wants to tell you something that happened at school today.

- Your parents tell you to be home by midnight. You are the only one of your friends who has a curfew.

- Your mother is telling her friends about something you did, and she gets one of the facts wrong.

- You want to borrow your sister's ice skates, and she's not home for you to ask permission.

- You promised your dad that you would help him clean the van at 2:00 P.M. It is 2:00, but you are just about to advance to the next level in your favorite video game.

- You cheat on a test at school and are caught. You feel angry with the teacher for calling your parents.

- You know that reverence in the chapel is a way to show respect for the Savior, but your friend keeps passing you notes.

Good conduct leads to self-respect; self-respect to respect for other people and property; and respect for people and property to good conduct. John Frederick William Herschel said it precisely: "Self-respect is the cornerstone of all virtue" (www.respectresearchgroup.org). When should you begin to set the example and provide formal and informal instruction on respect? Of course, the answer is "at the beginning," with those middle-of-the-night feedings. The answer is now.

TEACHING CHILDREN VIRTUE

In every dispensation, it has been important for parents to teach their children about virtue. Of course, I didn't live in any other dispensation, but it seems to me that due to the media in this dispensation of the fulness of times, ever so much more evil has come along with ever so much more revealed righteousness; therefore, a parent's responsibility appears to be even greater. Hopefully, some of the following will be helpful to you.

Step 1: Establish an open line of communication.

A young father, trying to help toilet train his two-year-old daughter and three-year-old son, made charts for them. Every success was rewarded with a sticker. Kathryn, age six, told her father that she'd like a chart too. He asked her what she wanted to work on. She said, "I'd like to stop sucking my thumb." The father gladly made her a chart. During the next week he talked to the three children individually about their successes during the day. Each day Kathryn reported that she had not sucked her thumb and was given a sticker. Her parents felt, however, that she was still sucking her thumb.

The next evening, as he was talking to Kathryn about how she had done that day, her father said, "I know that sucking your thumb is a hard habit to break. If you ever do suck your thumb, it's okay to tell me. I'd much rather have you tell me the truth, and I know it would make you feel bad if you told me that you didn't suck your thumb when you really did. How did you do today? Do you deserve a sticker?"

Kathryn said, "Just a minute, Daddy, I have to think about this," and left the room. It was several minutes before she returned. "Daddy,

I've sucked my thumb every day," she admitted. "Take off all my stickers."

Insightful parents set high standards but let their children feel comfortable in telling them the truth when they don't meet the parents' expectations. This is how open communication starts.

Step 2: Teach children to delay gratification.

You know the importance of teaching children to put off impulse and waiting to fulfill needs and wants. Remember the two marshmallows? Children who experience waiting for two marshmallows rather than receiving one immediately are much more likely to understand that chastity is worth the wait.

Step 3: Instill in each child an age-appropriate knowledge of the plan of salvation and the purpose of physical bodies.

The parenting principle of teaching pure doctrine is clearly shown in Alma 39–42 in which Alma instructs his son Corianton—who went off with a harlot while on a mission—in relevant principles of the gospel. *Doctrinal Commentary on the Book of Mormon* states:

> This points up a deeply significant principle—the value of teaching doctrine. One perusing these chapters might be prone to ask: "The boy has a moral problem; why preach to him? Why spend so much time discussing the spirit world, resurrection, judgment, the law of restoration, and the mercy and justice of God?" . . . As Elder Boyd K. Packer testified: "True doctrine, understood, changes attitudes and behavior. The study of the doctrines of the gospel will improve behavior quicker than a study of behavior will improve behavior. Preoccupation with unworthy behavior can lead to unworthy behavior. That is why we stress so forcefully the study of the doctrines of the gospel" (CR, October 1986, 20).
> (Joseph Fielding McConkie and Robert L. Millet, *Doctrinal Commentary on the Book of Mormon*, 3:321)

What is the doctrine? That procreation is the divine power of God. Doctrine and Covenants 132:15–18 teaches that those who are not worthy of a temple marriage will not be married in the eternities but will be "appointed angels in heaven, which angels are ministering servants, to minister for those who are worthy of a far more, and an exceeding, and an eternal weight of glory" (v. 16). Doctrine and Covenants 132:17 says "they cannot be enlarged [have children], but remain separately and singly . . . forever and ever."

Read also sections 76, 131, and 132 of the Doctrine and Covenants often and convey these precious doctrines to your children in a way that will encourage them to keep their minds and bodies pure. As the world rages in carnality, these truths must be taught and retaught at every age and stage.

Step 4: Teach what to do as well as what not to do.

If taught negatively, the gospel can seem like lists of "don't dos," especially with regard to use of the body. Most commandments, however, can be phrased in a positive way. For example: The reason to dress modestly is that your body is a gift from Heavenly Father that only followers of Christ received; it is, therefore, a sacred privilege. The scriptures teach how precious the gift of having a body is by the fact that Satan will never receive a body. He will never have a little son or daughter call him "Daddy." He and his followers want bodies so badly they are willing to share one man's body with legions of other evil spirits. They are even willing to have pigs' bodies (read the accounts in Matt. 8:28–32 and Mark 5:1–17).

Unfortunately, with today's availability of pornography and with evil portrayed as good and good as evil, parents are forced to use vocabulary and directness that in past eras wasn't as necessary. The Church has taken the lead in providing the pamphlet *For the Strength of Youth.* The teachings are explicit and are for parents as well as for the youth. I did a little survey of some mothers in my association who have teenagers and asked them how often their family home evening subject was on something to do with chastity. They all answered "at least once a month." One of our children said that his BYU bishop spoke on moral cleanliness every week. Getting a child safely to the temple takes inspiration and prayer and focus from parents, Church leaders, and teachers as never before.

Step 5: Exemplify what you teach.

How you revere your body is taught to your children from the moment of birth. Are you modest? Do you make exceptions and excuse certain of your own behaviors regarding use of your body? Do you speak respectfully about bodily functions? Do you avoid movies and television where themes or scenes are immoral? Do you hold in the highest regard marriage and birth, children and families? Do you show a healthy loving marital relationship between you and your husband as a role model?

Step 6: Teach the importance of the body?

President Spencer W. Kimball noted:

> The Lord said, "Be ye clean, that bear the vessels of the Lord" (Isaiah 52:11). And we must state and restate and call to the attention of our children and their children that chastity and cleanliness are basic in the Church. Parents should teach their children in their home evenings and in all their activities as they rear them that unchastity is a terrible sin, always has been, always will be and that no rationalization by any number of people will ever change it. As long as the stars shine in the heavens and the sun brings warmth to the earth and so long as men and women live upon this earth, there must be this holy standard of chastity and virtue. (Daniel H. Ludlow, *A Companion to Your Study of the Old Testament*, 305–6)

In an age when pornography is available at the click of a mouse, when coed dorms and unmarried couples living together are common, when sexuality is presented on the television and movie screen as a lifestyle of freedom and fun with no consequences attached, when abortion is touted as an easy alternative, even when kissing and more on the first date is routine, when little girls' fashions resemble Las Vegas nightlife, parents must teach that God abhors all sexuality outside of marriage. If all sexual sin were lumped together under the heading of one sin, it may be the sin of exploitation, which is mistreatment of, taking advantage of, or manipulation of another for personal gratification.

President Thomas S. Monson emphasized, "May I urge that each of us appreciate the significance of our temples and develop a love for them. President Spencer W. Kimball has long urged that in the bedroom of each Latter-day Saint child there [should] grace the wall a picture of the temple. As prayers are spoken, a sermon is before that boy, that girl—a gentle reminder from mother as the picture is viewed: 'Here you will marry'" (*Be Your Best Self*, 54–55). Hang a photo or painting of the temple in well-trafficked areas of your home. Go to the temple as often as possible. Share with your children how good you feel when you can answer the temple-recommend questions and humbly affirm, "Yes, I am worthy to enter the temple." Talk to your children about how they would feel if terrorists attacked the temple in your community. Help each understand that his or her body is a temple to be safeguarded and protected. Teach them that if they don't defile or pollute their bodies, they can have the Spirit of the Lord as a constant companion. Let them feel that you know that marriage in the temple and temple worthiness thereafter is the way to happiness in this life and joy throughout eternity. In word and deed, teach that the ultimate purpose of a physical body is to use it at the right time, with the right person, in the right way, with God's sanction, to give Heavenly Father's spirit children the opportunity of earth life. Believe me, I know this is no small task. But you can do it.

HOW DEAR TO GOD
ARE LITTLE CHILDREN

The Primary song "How Dear to God Are Little Children" is an affirmative statement, but the question is *how dear are little children to God?* President Spencer W. Kimball in *Faith Precedes the Miracle* quotes F. M. Bareham, whose thoughts give insight as to the value of children:

> [In 1809] men were following with baited breath the march of Napoleon and waiting with feverish impatience for news of the wars. And all the while in their homes babies were being born. But who could think about babies? Everybody was thinking about battles.

> In one year between Trafalgar and Waterloo there stole into the world a host of heroes: Gladstone was born in Liverpool; Tennyson at the Somersby Rectory; and Oliver Wendell Holmes in Massachusetts. Abraham Lincoln was born in Kentucky, and music was enriched by the advent of Felix Mendelssohn in Hamburg.

> But nobody thought of babies, everybody was thinking of battles. Yet which of the battles of 1809 mattered more than the babies of 1809? We fancy God can manage His world only with great battalions, when all the time he is doing it with beautiful babies.

When a wrong wants righting, or a truth wants preaching,
or a continent wants discovering, God sends a baby into
the world to do it. (323–24)

Every baby, every child deserves respect and opportunity. Not just
my children, not just children I am related to, not just the children in
my Primary class, not just the children of the Church, but every
child. Babies grow up to be children who grow up to be presidents
and prophets, musicians and scientists, mothers and fathers. You
know how Jesus treated little children from Bible and Book of
Mormon accounts. You know He admonishes everyone to become as
little children: "Verily I say unto you, Except ye be converted, and
become as little children, ye shall not enter into the kingdom of
heaven" (Matt. 18:3). Perhaps the most poignant moment in all scripture that teaches parents the value of their children comes in 3 Nephi
17:21–24, when Jesus "took their little children, one by one, and
blessed them, and prayed unto the Father for them." Then He wept
and said, "Behold your little ones." Angels descended, encircled, and
ministered to the children. When you take your children, one by one,
to bless them, to pray to the Father for them, you are following Jesus'
example. You are the angels who encircle them with protecting arms
and minister to them with caring hands. When I remind myself of
these sublime teachings, my love for little children increases.

Not only is Jesus' example important in understanding how dear
and precious little children are, but some of the most beautiful
doctrines in the gospel of Jesus Christ concern children and reinforce
their value. The Savior also warns parents that if they do not "teach
[their children] . . . to understand the doctrine of repentance, faith in
Christ the Son of the living God, and of baptism and the gift of the
Holy Ghost by the laying on of the hands, when eight years old, the
sin be upon the heads of the parents" (D&C 68:25). Of these imperative doctrines, baptism may be least understood.

Just in case you get interrupted and don't finish reading this paragraph, the following two incidents illustrate wrong principles. I was
in a sacrament meeting when a child who had just been baptized was
introduced by the bishop as "the cleanest person in the congregation."
Actually, all the little children who were not yet baptized were cleaner.

At a baptism, a counselor in the stake Primary presidency gave the baptism talk to the children who were about to be baptized. She held up a hard-boiled egg in her left hand and explained to the children that when they came to earth they were as clean as this egg. But when they told a lie (and she made a little scribble mark on the egg), or didn't obey a parent (she scribbled again), or did something unkind (another scribble), they needed to be baptized to wash their "wrongs" away. She then peeled the egg and showed them how clean they'd be after baptism. This is NOT correct doctrine. Children cannot sin until they reach the age of accountability.

The scriptures say, "Every spirit of man was innocent in the beginning; and God having redeemed man from the fall, men became again, in their infant state, innocent before God" (D&C 93:38). That's why in the restored gospel of Jesus Christ, children are not baptized at birth. Mormon, in Moroni 8, calls this sectarian idea of baptizing infants "a solemn mockery before God" (v. 9). He says, "I speak it boldly [as] God hath commanded me" (v. 21). "Little children are whole" (v. 8); "they are not capable of committing sin (v. 8); "little children cannot repent" (v.19); "little children are alive in Christ, even from the foundation of the world; if not so, God is a partial God, and also a changeable God, and a respecter to persons; for how many little children have died without baptism!" (v.12); "behold I say unto you, that he that supposeth that little children need baptism is in the gall of bitterness and in the bonds of iniquity; . . . [It is] awful . . . wickedness to suppose that God saveth one child because of baptism, and the other must perish because he hath no baptism" (vv. 14–15); "[The baptism of little children] availeth nothing" (v. 22).

Since "[little children] cannot sin, for power is not given unto Satan to tempt little children, until they begin to become accountable before me," (D&C 29:47), how are children's "wrongs" made right? You already know the answer. It's through the Atonement. It's through the Atonement of Christ that all men, women, and children will be saved (see A of F 3). Teach your children, as early as possible but certainly before age eight, that baptism is for the remission of sins after a person is eight years old. Before age eight, he or she is covered by Jesus' infinite love for little children. Teach your children that their baptism at age eight is for the purpose of being obedient, as Jesus was.

He had no sin but was baptized "to fulfill all righteousness" (JST—Matt. 3:43). Children know the Savior loves them and will want to be baptized to follow His example. He was sinless, and they are sinless because of His Atonement. Teach your children about the age of accountability and how to repent. They should feel sorry for the bad things they do and learn to make restitution. Children will realize that after baptism, at whatever age, everyone needs to repent and seek forgiveness. Teach them about the importance of the sacrament in the repentance process.

The doctrine found in Doctrine and Covenants 137:10 gives assurance that all children who die under the age of eight inherit the celestial kingdom: "I . . . beheld that all children who die before they arrive at the years of accountability are saved in the celestial kingdom of heaven." This same doctrine holds true for those whose mental ability never allows them to reach a state of accountability, both for baptism and death. What comforting doctrine!

> *How dear to God are little children;*
> *With Him their spirit life began.*
> *So priceless their security, Their innocence and purity;*
> *They are a part of his eternal plan.*
>
> *To earthly parents God sends children*
> *To guide and teach, protect and love.*
> *Oh, let us keep the sacred trust That He has placed with each of us*
> *And help to guide them back to God above.*
> ("How Dear to God Are Little Children," *Children's Songbook,* 180–81)

NEEDS AND BALANCE BEAMS

If you are young, old, or in between, married, divorced, single, employed, stay-at-home, childless, or the mother of many, you have needs. Walking the care-for-yourself balance beam of life is tricky.

You can easily become self-absorbed and so overly concerned with your own looks, health, rights, intellect, leisure, talents (the list is endless), that you fall off the balance beam, figuratively to the left. Or you can be too sacrificial, revel in being a victim or martyr, and savor your suffering too often and for too long. Or you can live in denial to the reality that you do have needs. When these feelings become extreme, you fall off the balance beam, figuratively to the right.

But whether you fall off to the right or the left doesn't matter, because either way you fall. And both are actually the same problem—self-absorption—just different manifestations. Both ways you are caught up in your own importance.

The hardest part of staying on the balance beam is that everyone's balancing ability is different and everyone's balance beam is different. Your beam, the one with your name on it, was made to build your physical endurance, your emotional stamina, and your spiritual alacrity. The awareness that is essential to staying on the beam comes when you realize that no balance beam is smooth. Every life has obstacles and adversities. When you internalize the fact that the obstacles and adversities are not interruptions to life but the very core and essence of life, then you can walk your beam with more confidence.

Below are five areas of concern that each woman must balance in order to stay on her beam as much as possible. Each is important and intertwined. You can't be balanced in just one area. The goal is to be as whole and complete as mortality allows.

The delicate part of this balancing act is that life is ever changing. Being balanced is ongoing. What worked yesterday might not work as well today. The purpose of this lesson is to inspire you to reach a little deeper and do a little better in at least one area.

Spiritual Balance

Prayer, scripture study, fasting, keeping the commandments, and temple attendance are some common aspects of spiritual balancing. Which is most important to you right now? The answer is, of course, the one you struggle with the most. Meditate on your spiritual strengths and weaknesses. Ask yourself what prevents you from being more spiritual? Decide on one way you want to improve. Write it down in the form of a goal.

Physical Balance

How could you be more physically balanced? Do you need to exercise, lose weight, get to bed earlier, follow your doctor's advice, eat more nutritionally, kick an unhealthy habit? Ask yourself: What prevents me from feeling more vigorous and healthy? Decide on one way you want to improve. Write it down in the form of a goal.

Emotional Balance

It is hard to overstate the importance of emotional health. The more emotionally balanced you are the better everything else is. Do you see life as it really is and in perspective? Can you self-credit and self-correct? Are you self-disciplined? Do you have fears that are keeping you from the balance you desire? Think about what prevents you from being more emotionally vigorous and acting in consistent, healthy ways. Decide on one way you want to improve, and write it down in the form of a goal.

Interpersonal Relationship Balance

The ability to nurture others, to live in gratitude, to give service, to feel empathy, and to see life from others' perspectives are all vital. What are your interpersonal relationship strengths and weaknesses?

Could you be a better listener, more patient, more empathetic, more understanding, more helpful, more courageous? Decide on one way you want to improve and write it down in the form of a goal.

Personal Fulfillment Balance

How much time, energy, and resources should you give to developing your talents and interests in your current stage of life? Should you do more or less? Meditate on how you can enrich yourself and others, remembering that sometimes less is more. Decide on an area of focus. Write it down in the form of a goal.

Look at your five goals. Pray about which should be your primary concern and write sub-goals to help you make changes to meet those goals. Anticipate as you inch along your beam; you may stutter step, misstep, even step backward now and then. Sometimes you might fall off the beam and land ungracefully and, on occasion, injure yourself.

But your Heavenly Father watches you as you navigate along your balance beam. He gave you your life. You are His child. He gave you His Son whose grace makes up for your lack of grace. He provides a member of the Godhead who can be your constant companion. This is His plan and He will support you on the beam when you wobble or fall either to the right or the left. For He said: "I will go before your face. I will be on your right hand and on your left, and my Spirit shall be in your hearts, and mine angels round about you, to bear you up" (D&C 84:88).

FAMILY PECAN TREES

Elder Carlos E. Asay wrote a book in 1992 titled *Family Pecan Trees*. In the prologue he introduces the title and focus of the book by quoting an article from *U.S. News and World Report* (June 13, 1977, 84):

> On the plains of Texas and Oklahoma, where trees are sometimes rare and precious things, there is a tradition that recognizes the responsibility of one generation for the next.
>
> Rural homesteaders, once the house was built, the well dug and the first few crops harvested, would plant their "grandchildren grove."
>
> Laboriously, the farmer would read a score or more of seed catalogues and finally select a particular type of pecan tree. It had to be hard and strong, able to withstand the deep winters and torrid summers of those dry plains. He would make his selection and send off carefully hoarded money.
>
> In due time, a tree, hardly larger than a switch, would arrive. The farmer would place roots of the dry and unpromising stick in water and then dig a hole, deep and wide. Tenderly, he would plant the tree, packing the soil firmly about its roots. Then he would water it, carrying bucketful after bucketful from his well.

If he did his job well, in the spring—wonders of all wonders—the stick would sprout leaves.

Over the years, he would plant others and carefully tend them. But it wouldn't be for his benefit, because pecan trees grow very slowly, inching their way upward.

To some it seemed folly, for the farmer would be dead and gone long before the grove he planted could provide substantial shade or a harvest of the sweet-meated nuts.

But there was a saying that explained: "Plant corn for yourself and pecans for your grandchildren."

Some farmers felt work that went unrewarded for generations was a waste. Instead of pecans, they planted plum trees that grew quickly and soon produced fat, juicy fruit. For a decade or two, the plum trees did well, but eventually their soft wood split, and from the roots sprouted plum bushes that eventually became a snarl of scraggly, unproductive branches.

Just what are you planting in the hearts and minds of your children? That question is appropriate every day because your busyness and mine may confuse what is essential with what is trivial, what is important with what is fluff, what is true with what is traditional, what is lasting with what is fleeting, what is central with what is peripheral. It's easier to think short-term than long-term because it is imperative to have the essential corn, and many aspects of life are made nicer by sweet juicy plums. But wisdom necessitates that some pecan trees get planted along the way.

Images of sowing and harvesting, of trees bearing fruit, of gardeners, vines, branches, and roots fill sacred writ. Alma 32:28–43 compares the planting of a seed to testimony. And Jesus said, "By their fruits ye shall know them" (Matt. 7:20). The most important part of all this is to plant. Yet farmers know that planting is only the beginning. They don't plant and go on vacation, thinking their work is done. They plant to harvest. Plant for today, tomorrow, and to cross generations. Pass on a bounteous legacy. Plant in the souls of your children the principles of faith, love, knowledge, obedience, and testimony by your example of:

- Light—plant light by being a light. Stress, hurry, worry, and fatigue dull the light of your personality and the light of your testimony. Be a light to your family and friends by radiating and reflecting the light of the Savior. It was He who said, "Let there be light" (Gen. 1:3).

- Gratitude—plant gratitude by showing and expressing appreciation. Express your gratefulness to Heavenly Father. "Give thanks unto the Lord, call upon his name, make known his deeds among the people" (1 Chron. 16:8). Convey to your family your gratitude for Heavenly Father, for Jesus Christ, and for the Holy Ghost. Show gratitude for the restored gospel by remembering the prophet of the Restoration, Joseph Smith. Show love and appreciation for our living prophet today.

- Faith—plant faith by showing that your optimism and testimony in the good times stays constant in adversity. The Apostle Paul wrote, "We are troubled on every side, yet not distressed; we are perplexed, but not in despair; Persecuted, but not forsaken; cast down, but not destroyed" (2 Cor. 4:8–9). Remember that faith is things hoped for, not things that are. Faith is always a projection into the future. "For we walk by faith, not by sight" (2 Cor. 5:7). Study about faith in Ether 12 and in Moroni 7.

- Smiling—plant safety, contentment, appreciation, and love in the world by smiling. When everyone is in a hurry and time is running short, take a deep breath and smile. Turn up the corners of your mouth. Smile at each family member many times each day. Smile at yourself in the mirror. I have a friend whose husband died a violent death. When I went to see her some time after the funeral, she was contentedly going about her work. I asked her how she could possibly be okay. In essence she told me that she had analyzed her situation and thought she'd never smile again. But then the idea came to her that she should try smiling, and somehow in the act of smiling, she began to feel at peace. Though I am not intimating that simply smiling will lift your heaviest burdens, we should follow the Lord's command to "be of good cheer" (D&C 61:36) amidst our trials. It is part of having faith. While the common belief is that you smile when you are happy, you might want to view it as the other way around. Smile, and then you will be happy.

Plant with light, gratitude, faith, and a happy face, and some future grandchild of yours may write about the family pecan trees you planted: "On the plains of (wherever you live), where trees are sometimes rare and precious things, my grandparents recognized the responsibility of one generation for the next and planted pecan trees, and the harvest is great."

THEME INDEX

PHOTO BY JOHN W. LINFORD

ABOUT THE AUTHOR

Marilynne Todd Linford is a nature lover, people watcher, amateur philosopher, and breast cancer survivor. She and her husband Richard are parents of eight and grandparents of nineteen. Marilynne has written seven other books: *ABC's for Young LDS, I Hope They Call Me on a Mission Too!, Is Anyone Out There Building Mother's Self-Esteem?, Slim for Life, Breast Cancer—Support Group in a Book, A Woman Fulfilled,* and *Give Mom a Standing Ovation.* Her hobbies include playing piano duets and/or Scrabble with anyone who is willing, studying LDS Church history, being a docent at the Church Museum of History and Art, and most of all enjoying her family.

If you would like to correspond with Marilynne, please send an e-mail to info@covenant-lds.com. You may also write to her in care of Covenant Communications, P.O. Box 416, American Fork, UT 84003-0416.